PATCHWORK
& QUILTING

Memorable Scrap Quilts

Craftworld Books

Contents

Making Do Makes Memories

From the necessary thrift of hard times has grown a wonderful
style of patchwork which is actually made of memories – and a true heirloom.

Text by Justyna Lupa

Scrap quilts not only have a wonderful homely charm but they embody the old-fashioned virtues of frugality and making do. These are not the beautiful quilts that win Best of Show awards – they are the quilts we wrap our young ones in when they have the flu, and in which we ourselves snuggle up on cold winter nights.

Traditionally many quilts were made using scraps of fabric too good to throw away, as Deborah Harding describes in the book Quilts:

"THE PIONEER ETHIC STRESSED THE USE OF EVERY SCRAP OF FABRIC, NO MATTER HOW SMALL. PURCHASING NEW YARDAGE FOR A QUILT TOP WAS A LAST RESORT; TRUE INGENUITY WAS A MATTER OF RECYCLING FABRICS."

"In addition to cast-off clothing received from family members or garnered from thrift shops, feed sacks, sugar sacks, and tobacco and flour sacks were all saved, cut, bleached, and dyed for use in quilts".

In many ways the scrap quilt represents the way patchwork began. And the many antique scrap quilts that have survived to this day are testament to the 'pioneer ethic' Deborah mentions. In the book Scrap Quilts – The Art of Making Do, Roberta Horton wrote: "Antique scrap quilts can be the most humble of quilts and, at the same time, the most complicated of all quilts to understand ... Scrap quilts were made to be used. They were unpretentious and honest – and, at the same time, beautiful."

Scrap quilts have come from a long tradition which Australian quilters have wholeheartedly embraced, and making one of these quilts is always a satisfying task as well as a great exercise in recycling. It also provides the perfect opportunity to use up those scraps which have been discarded from other projects.

Many scrap quilts aren't elaborate and often the best ones are made using a traditional block repeated in an assortment of fabrics. There are many types of popular blocks which quilters use for their scrap quilts, one of the most popular being the Log Cabin block.

Elizabeth V. Warren and Sharon L. Eisenstat wrote in Glorious American Quilts: "Just as the log dwelling has long been considered a symbol of American spirit and courage – so, too, has the Log Cabin quilt often been seen as the archetypal American bedcover." Log Cabin quilts were – and still are – popular in Australia with many examples still in existence from as far back as the 1890s.

Many quilters begin their quiltmaking journey with this special type of quilt and the Log Cabin block makes an ideal scrap quilt because it uses small pieces of fabric in light, medium and dark colours.

From Log Cabin quilts came a similar style of quilts called String quilts. These quilts were made using leftover fabric that was too small to be used anywhere else, even in a Log Cabin quilt.

Another type of scrap quilt – albeit in a much more exotic style – are crazy quilts which were popular during the late 1800s. These quilts were inspired by England's Arts and Crafts Movement, led by the well-known designer, William Morris. These quilts were also inspired by the oriental designs popular in Europe when regular trade with Asia became established. Traditionally, crazy quilts weren't made by pioneer women but by wealthy women who had enough leisure time to make these pieces which were more decorative than functional.

One example of a stunning Australian

"SCRAP QUILTS WERE MADE TO BE USED. THEY WERE UNPRETENTIOUS AND HONEST — AND, AT THE SAME TIME, BEAUTIFUL."

It's not uncommon for quilters to use scraps from clothes they have made or ones that are worn out or even children's old clothes.

A truly traditional Australian type of scrap quilt is the 'wagga' which was made during the Second World War. Due to shortages and rationing, goods such as fabric were limited and many had to make do with whatever scraps they had. Many waggas were simply made with strips of any available fabrics including woollen jumpers, blankets and cotton cretonne which were all sewn together and then – with no batting available – the quilts were stuffed with old clothes and blankets.

Waggas were first thought to have been made around Wagga Wagga in Southern NSW, a major wheat producing area and it's believed that these quilts were made using wheat sacks filled with old woollen clothing for warmth. In her book Patchwork Quilts in Australia, Margaret Rolfe writes: "Originally made by men and used outdoors, a wagga rug was associated with shearers and bushmen. In his story 'The Darling River', published in 1893, Henry Lawson mentions shearers having them: "The live cinders from the firebox… fell in showers on deck. Every now and then a spark would burn through the 'Wagga rug' of a sleeping shearer, and he'd wake up suddenly and get up and curse'."

Another wonderful tradition in scrap quilts involved those made from military uniforms. These quilts weren't made in khaki green which is the common colours of military uniforms today but out of the rich dress uniforms popular before the Boer War. As Margaret describes in

crazy patchwork quilt was made by Marion Gibson in the late 1800s which was featured in Margaret Rolfe's book, Australian Quilt Heritage . Margaret wrote that when Marion was bequeathing the quilt to her grand-daughter she wrote a letter about what the quilt meant to her. "She wrote of how 'it was all made with pieces from friends far and near. I called it the "Friendship quilt", and to me it was a labour of love'. The pieces of fabric evoked memories of the givers, some coming from her family back in Scotland. There were pieces of wedding dresses from family and friends, baby ribbons, her own ribbons, pieces of dresses and neckties. 'Ties are well represented' she wrote, 'one your uncle Bob bought from Melbourne, and there is one of old Mr Budd, an early squatter. I put it beside one of your Grandfather's, so I went in for "Federation" on that "quilt" – for all classes are united'."

Crazy quilts don't symbolise thrift or frugality but they symbolise another endearing aspect of scrap quilts and that is with the collection of fabrics. The use of memorable pieces of fabric such as Marion used in her quilt is a practice still popular with many quilters today. Because scrap quilts use so many different fabrics they become a treasure trove of memories.

because they love the sheer simplicity and prefer the spontaneity of not having to coordinate everything. And, because many quilters are self-confessed fabric addicts, scrap quilts provide the ideal way to use up as many fabrics as possible.

Further Reading
- ❧ *Patchwork Quilts in Australia by Margaret Rolfe, Greenhouse, Victoria, 1987.*
- ❧ *Australian Quilt Heritage by Margaret Rolfe, J.B. Fairfax Press Pty Ltd, Sydney 1998.*
- ❧ *Scrap Quilts – The Art of Making Do by Roberta Hortan, C&T Publishing, California, 1998*
- ❧ *Glorious American Quilts by Elizabeth V. Warren and Sharon L. Eisenstat, Penguin Group, New York, 1996.*
- ❧ *Quilts by Dennis Duke and Deborah Harding, Könemann, Köln, 1996.*

Patchwork Quilts in Australia, "the making of uniforms, especially dress uniforms, would have provided a rich source of colourful woollen fabrics." There are few of these quilts in Australia but one stunning example is in Tasmania, by Millist Vincent who was a soldier in the Boer War.

The thrifty home-maker had many other sources of acquiring fabric for quilts. Antique quilts often include rich fabrics such as silks, velvets, ribbons and also more common fabrics such as clothing and even woollen suiting samples. In the times when fabric was scarce, it seems, creativity was high and where there was a will there was sure to be a way.

These days, fabrics for quilts are much easier to come by, but the spirit of scrap quilts lives on. There are many craft shops which specialise in patchwork, but there are also many quilters who still use their ingenuity and creativity to acquire fabric for their patchwork projects.

One wonderful scrap tradition is the 'charm' swaps that many quilters participate in. These are usually organised within quilting groups and now, there are also many international forums for quilters

to meet and swap fabric on the Internet.

Many quilters make scrap quilts

Happy Birthday

This surprisingly easy-to-stitch quilt features Star blocks and Puss in Corner blocks, and was made by Jennifer Stanley for a favourite aunt's 70th birthday.

CUTTING

❖

From the background, cut:

– 21, 2¹⁄₂in strips and crosscut 72, 2¹⁄₂in squares and 144, 2¹⁄₂in x 4¹⁄₂in rectangles for the pieced blocks

– three, 3¹⁄₂in strips and crosscut 25, 3¹⁄₂in squares. Cut these twice on the diagonal to yield 100 triangles for the second border

– four, 2¹⁄₂in squares for the cornerstones in the second border.

From the assorted blue prints, cut:

– 352, 2¹⁄₂in squares for the pieced blocks

– 26, 3¹⁄₂in squares, cut these twice on the diagonal to yield 102 triangles for the second border.

From the medium blue second border fabric, cut:

– four, 2⁷⁄₈in strips and crosscut 48, 2⁷⁄₈in squares, cut these once on the diagonal to yield 96 triangles for the second border

– one, 3¹⁄₂in square, cut twice on the diagonal for the second border.

From the first border fabric, cut:

– five, 1¹⁄₂in strips.

From the third border fabric, cut:

– seven, 4¹⁄₂in strips

– seven, 2¹⁄₂in strips for the binding.

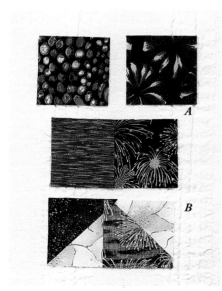

BLOCK CONSTRUCTION

❖

BLOCK A

A total of 18 Block A is required. Stitch together 72, assorted blue 2¹⁄₂in squares to yield 36 pairs. Following photograph 1, (A) stitch these units together to form 18 four-patch units.

Using 72 background rectangles and 144, 2¹⁄₂in assorted blue squares, make 72 star units for the blocks. Rule a diagonal line across the 2¹⁄₂in squares. Using photograph 2 (B) as a guide, place the 2¹⁄₂in square right sides together with the background rectangle and stitch across the diagonal. Trim away the excess blue fabric and press the blue triangle towards the corner.

Stitch a background 2¹⁄₂in square to the opposite ends of the 36 star points. Press the seams towards the star points.

Stitch the remaining 36 star points to either side of 18 of your scrap four-patch units. Press the seams towards the star points. Lay out the completed units as shown in photograph 2 and stitch.

BLOCK B

A total of 17 block B is required. Stitch together 68, assorted blue 2¹⁄₂in squares to yield 34 pairs. Following photograph 1, stitch these units together to form 17 four-patch units.

Using photograph 3 as a guide, stitch a 2¹⁄₂in blue square to each end of 34, 2¹⁄₂in x 4¹⁄₂in rectangles. Press the seams towards the blue squares.

Sew the remaining 34 background rectangles to either side of the four-patch units. Press the seams away from the background rectangle.

Photograph 1. A. *Stitch together 72, assorted blue 2¹⁄₂in squares to yield 36 pairs. Stitch these units together to form a four patch unit.* ***B.*** *Place the 2¹⁄₂in square right sides together with the background rectangle and stitch across the diagonal.*

MATERIALS

• 2.3m (2¹⁄₂yd) light cream background fabric

• 30cm (¹⁄₃yd) 15 different blue fabrics for star points etc; or enough scraps to cut 352, 2¹⁄₂in squares and 26, 3¹⁄₂in squares

• 30cm (¹⁄₃yd) dark blue for the first border

• 40cm (¹⁄₂yd) medium blue for the second border

• 1.5m (1²⁄₃yd) dark blue for third border and binding

• 3m (3¹⁄₃yd) backing fabric

• 1.5m x 2.3m (1²⁄₃yd x 2¹⁄₂yd) batting

• Cotton thread for piecing

• Clear monofilament and embroidery thread for quilting

• Rotary cutter, ruler and mat

• Sewing machine with a ¹⁄₄in foot

FINISHED QUILT SIZE

137cm x 177cm (54in x 70in)

FINISHED BLOCK SIZE

20cm (8in) square

NOTE: It is recommended that fabrics be 100 per cent cotton, pre-washed and ironed. Requirements are based on fabric 112cm (44in wide). Seam allowances of ¹⁄₄in are used and are included in the rotary cutting instructions.

Lay out the completed units as shown in photograph 3 and stitch them together.

QUILT ASSEMBLY

❖

Using the quilt layout diagram as a guide, stitch the blocks together alternating block A and block B. Jenny recommends when joining block A to the alternate block, wherever possible sew from the star side where the star point sewing lines have crossed. This makes it easy to see exactly where the stitching line needs to be to give you perfect points.

FIRST BORDER

❖

Trim two strips to $40\frac{1}{2}$in and stitch them to the top and bottom of quilt top, pin-marking the top and bottom edges of the quilt top and the border strips into quarters. Stitch them together matching the pin-markings and press the seams towards the border. Sew the remaining three border strips together to form one long length and trim two, $58\frac{1}{2}$in strips. Stitch these to the opposite sides of the quilt top in the same manner as before, and press the seams toward border.

SECOND BORDER

❖

A total of 48, unit A; 48, unit B; four, unit C and four cornerstones are required.

UNIT A

Using diagram 1 as a guide, stitch each of 48 assorted blue triangles to a background triangle. Stitch these to a second border triangle to create unit A.

Photograph 2. *Stitch a $2\frac{1}{2}$in blue square to each end of 34, $4\frac{1}{2}$in x $2\frac{1}{2}$in rectangles. Press the seams towards the blue squares.*

Photograph 3. *Stitch a $2\frac{1}{2}$in blue square to each of 34, $2\frac{1}{2}$in x $4\frac{1}{2}$in rectangle.*

Quilt layout diagram

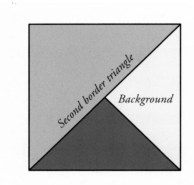

Diagram 1. *Stitch each of 48 assorted blue triangles to a background triangle. Stitch these to a second border triangle.*

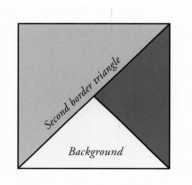

Diagram 2. *Stitch each of 48 assorted blue triangles to a background triangle. Stitch these to a second border triangle.*

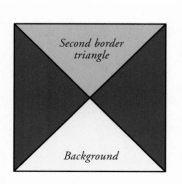

Diagram 3. *Unit C, stitch two assorted blue triangles together with a background and second border triangle.*

UNIT B

Stitch each of 48 assorted blue triangles to a background triangle, using diagram 2 as a guide. Stitch these to a second border triangle to create unit B. Using diagram 3 as a guide, stitch two assorted blue triangles together with a background and second border triangle to make each of the four centre border units. Lay out the second border units using the quilt layout diagram as guide. Stitch the units together to form the borders, then stitch them to the quilt top, pin-marking these in the same manner as the first border.

THIRD BORDER

❖

Stitch the 4$\frac{1}{2}$in third border strips together into one long length and trim two, 62$\frac{1}{2}$in lengths and two 54$\frac{1}{2}$in strips. Stitch the 62$\frac{1}{2}$in strips to the opposite sides of quilt top and press the seams towards the border. Stitch the 54$\frac{1}{2}$in strips to the top and bottom of the quilt top again pressing the seams towards the border.

BACKING

❖

Cut the length of backing fabric into two equal lengths and join them along the selvedge with a wide seam to make a backing for the quilt with one horizontal seam. Remove the selvedges and press the seam to one side.

Working on a large, flat surface, layer the backing right side down with the batting and quilt top right side up. Smooth the layers from the centre outwards to remove any wrinkles as you go, then baste the three layers together, ensuring the surfaces remain even. Use safety pins to baste for machine-quilting or thread if you have chosen to quilt by hand.

QUILTING

❖

Jenny has machine-quilted using monofilament thread in-the-ditch around all star points and blue scrap squares, pieced border, and she has stipple-quilted the background using matching machine-embroidery thread. The third border has been quilted with a continuous heart design in matching thread.

BINDING

❖

Sew the seven strips together using 45-degree seams to make one continuous length and press the seams open.

Press the long sides in half with wrong sides together.

Press a $\frac{1}{4}$in hem at the beginning of the binding strip.

Attach it to the quilt, beginning halfway down one side and leaving a 3in tail before you begin stitching. Using a $\frac{1}{4}$in seam allowance, sew around the quilt mitring each corner as you go.

When you are almost back to the beginning cut off the excess and slip the remainder under the hem of the open tail and continue stitching through all thicknesses until you reach the start.

Trim the excess backing and batting then turn the folded side over to the back of the quilt and slip-stitch it in place by hand.

Attach a label with the title of your quilt, your name, the date and any other relevant information – for example if the quilt is a gift for anyone special, as this quilt was. ✳

Jenny teaches appliqué, piecing and quilting-all by machine and may be contacted on (02) 4951 3753.

Cubic Puzzler

*With a new twist on traditional blocks, Susan Murphy has designed
her Cubic Puzzler with three-dimensional folded corners which appear
complex but are deceptively easy to piece.*

CUTTING

❖

Divide the assorted scrap fabrics into light and dark values. From the dark-value fabrics cut:

– 25, 2½in squares, one square for each block centre
– 50, 2in x 2½in rectangles, two rectangles for each block
– 100, 2in x 5½in rectangles, four rectangles for each block
– 50, 2in x 8½in rectangles, two rectangles for each block
– 60, 2in x 8½in strips for the sashings.

From the light-value fabrics cut:

– 200, 2½in squares, eight squares for the folded corners of each block
– 36, 2in squares for the corner squares of the sashings.

BLOCK CONSTRUCTION

❖

The quilt is made from 25 blocks. To make each block, following photograph 1, join two, 2in x 2½in rectangles to opposite sides of the 2½in centre square and press the seam allowances towards the outside of the block.

Join one, 2in x 5½in rectangle to each of the two remaining sides of the block and carefully press. Then fold four, 2½in light-value squares in half diagonally and, following photograph 2, pin the triangles formed to the corners of the pieced unit making sure that all the raw edges are aligned.

In the same manner as the preceding rectangles, add two, 2in x 5½in rectangles and then two, 2in x 8½in rectangles to the block incorporating the folded triangles into the seams as shown in photograph 3. Fold another four, 2½in squares and pin these to the corners of the block in the same manner as the other triangles.

These triangles will be stitched in the seams joining the blocks and the sashings, however, if preferred the blocks can be edge-stitched ⅛in inside the seam allowance so the pins can be removed as shown in photograph 4.

ASSEMBLY

❖

Arrange the 25 blocks into five rows of five blocks on a design wall or a floor. Distribute the blocks so that eye-catching fabrics are spread out evenly throughout the quilt rather than all being concentrated in the one area.

Following the photograph of the quilt, place the 60, 2in x 8½in sashing strips and the 36, 2in corner squares for the sashing between and around the blocks. Once again, make sure that the fabrics are evenly distributed.

Using the photograph of the quilt as a guide, make six horizontal rows of alternating corner squares and sashing strips. Making sure to start and end each row with a corner square.

Starting with a sashing strip and alternating with the pieced blocks, make five horizontal rows, each containing six sashing strips and five pieced blocks. Then carefully press all the seams towards the sashing strips.

Join the rows, abutting the seams together at the intersections, to form the quilt top, then press it.

BORDERS

❖

FIRST BORDER

From the full width of the cream fabric for the first border cut:

– three, 1½in strips and
– three, 2½in strips.

MATERIALS

• A wide variety of assorted scrap fabrics
• 40cm (½yd) of cream fabric for the first border
• 1m (1⅛yd) of printed fabric for the second border and the quilt binding
• 3.4m (3⅝yd) of backing fabric
• 163cm (64in) square of batting
• Neutral-coloured thread for piecing
• Quilting thread
• 2 skeins of black embroidery floss
• Pencil
• Rotary cutter, quilter's ruler and mat
• Sewing machine
• General sewing supplies

FINISHED BLOCK SIZE

20.5cm (8in)

FINISHED QUILT SIZE

146cm x 149cm (57½in x 58½in)

NOTE: It is recommended that fabrics be 100 per cent cotton, pre-washed and ironed. Material requirements are based on fabric 112cm (44in) wide. Cutting requirements include ¼in seam allowances.

Photograph 1. *Join rectangles to two opposite sides of the centre square and press the seam allowances towards the outside of the block. Join rectangles to the two remaining sides of the block.*

Photograph 2. Fold four squares in half diagonally and pin the triangles formed to the four corners of the pieced unit aligning all the raw edges.

Photograph 3. Add two, 2in x 5¹⁄₂in rectangles and then two, 2in x 8¹⁄₂in rectangles to the block, incorporating the folded triangles into the seams.

Photograph 4. Fold another four, 2¹⁄₂in squares and pin these to the four corners of the block.

Join the sets of strips into two long lengths. Measure the length of the quilt top through the centre and cut two strips of this measurement from the narrower strip.

Pin mark the two sides of the quilt top and the strips into quarters and join the strips to the quilt making sure that the pins are matched. Press the seams towards the borders.

Measure the width of the quilt top through the centre, cut two strips to this measurement and join these to the top and bottom of the quilt in the same manner.

The pattern for Susan's embroidery is printed on the pattern sheet.

Transfer the words onto the top and bottom borders of the quilt top and then transfer the looped lines onto the two side borders. Stitch the embroidery with two strands of thread.

When the embroidery has been completed, press the quilt top.

SECOND BORDER

From the full width of the fabric for the second border cut:

– six, 3¹⁄₂in strips.

Join these strips into two lengths, each with three strips.

Measure the width of the quilt top through the centre and join the second border to it in the same manner as the first border. Then carefully press.

BACKING

Cut the length of backing fabric in half and from one of the lengths cut two strips, 12in wide. Remove the selvedges and join one, 12in strip to either side of the full-width piece to make a backing a little larger than the quilt with two vertical joins. Press the seams open.

Layer the quilt top, the batting and the backing together, making sure that you smooth out each layer as you go. Pin or baste the three layers together.

QUILTING

Susan's quilt has been machine-quilted with a curved design at the centre of each block and in the outer border. The borders have been quilted in the ditch.

BINDING

From the remaining fabric for the outer border and binding cut:

– six, 2¹⁄₂in strips.

Join the strips into one long length with bias joins and press the seams open. Press the length of binding in half with wrong sides together.

Beginning approximately halfway along one side, join the binding to the quilt with a ¹⁄₄in seam, mitring at each corner. Trim the excess batting and backing fabric leaving a small excess of approximately ¹⁄₄in, turn the folded edge of the binding to the back of the quilt and hand-stitch it in place. Add a label to the back of your quilt including details of any special fabrics used as well as your name and the date the quilt was completed. ✳

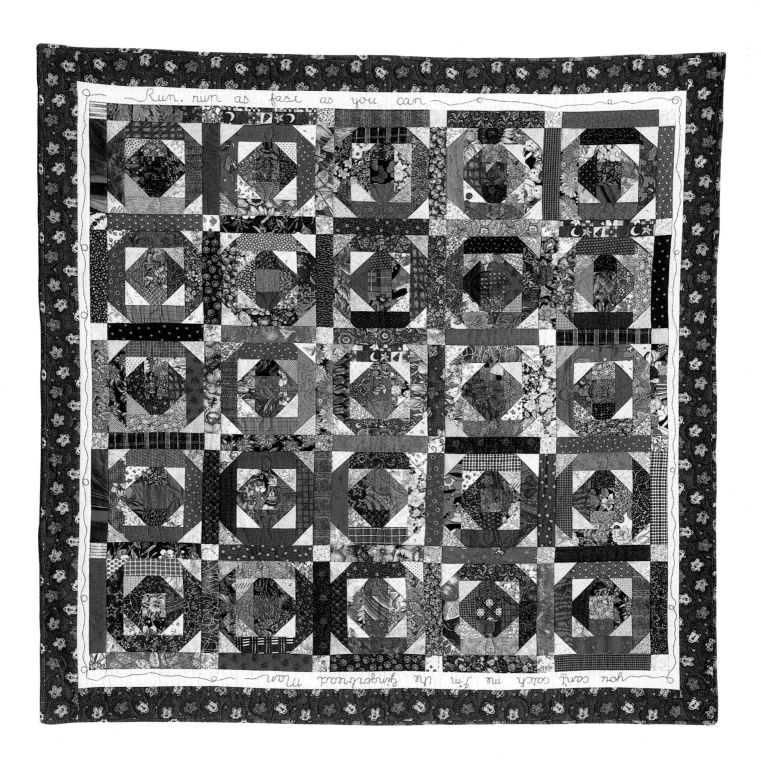

Dancing Dollies Bag

Cindy Cudmore always admired the Dancing Dollies block and after seeing an antique quilt from Ayres Historic House with its endearing dolly design, she knew she had to use the block in a project of her own.

CUTTING

❖

From the width of the striped fabric, cut:
- one, $10\frac{1}{2}$in x 32in rectangle for the main bag piece
- two, 2in strips and trim two 31in strips for the handles
- one, 1in x 18in strip for the tab.

From blue print fabric, cut:
- two, $2\frac{1}{2}$in strips and trim two 37in strips for the binding
- four, 2in strips and trim them to 31in strips for the handles
- one, $9\frac{1}{2}$in x 14in rectangle for the base
- two, 1in x 18in strips for the tab
- the remainder of the blue print fabric is set aside for the scallops.

From the lining fabric, cut:
- one, $10\frac{1}{2}$in x 33in rectangle
- one, $9\frac{1}{2}$in x 14in rectangle for base.

From fusible batting cut:
- one, $10\frac{1}{2}$in x 32in rectangle for the bag
- one, $9\frac{1}{2}$in x 14in rectangle for the base
- six, $\frac{3}{4}$in x 31in strips for the handles.

APPLIQUE

❖

Using the pattern provided on the pattern sheet, trace the appliqué shapes onto the paper side of the fusible web. Note that the head overlaps the doll's dress by approximately $\frac{1}{8}$in. The dress and scallops both extend to the raw edges at the bottom and top of the bag. A seam allowance of $\frac{1}{4}$in has been included on the pattern sheet.

Trace six dresses, six heads, 12 sets of arms, five hearts and two half-hearts with $\frac{1}{4}$in seam allowance added. Two lengths of 17 full scallops with half a scallop at each end, and the $\frac{1}{4}$in seam allowance measures 32in.

Cut out each of the shapes about $\frac{1}{4}$in in from the traced line. Then, iron the shapes onto the wrong side of the selected fabrics.

To make the two-colour hearts, cut a $1\frac{1}{2}$in x 7in strip from each of the six dress fabrics. Using a $\frac{1}{8}$in seam, sew a blue and a yellow strip together lengthwise. For the third pair, sew the seam only halfway along the length. Carefully press the seams open.

Using photograph 1 as a guide, centre the middle of the fusible-web heart over the seamline and press, making sure you turn the second heart so it appears upside down. On the third strip, iron the full heart in place and the two half-hearts – making sure you include the $\frac{1}{4}$in seam allowance. Cut out the pieces on the traced line and remove the backing paper.

On the main bag fabric, pin-mark a $\frac{1}{4}$in seam at each end of the rectangle. Mark six, $5\frac{1}{4}$in segments between the pin-markings. Use these as a guide to position the dresses, then following the pattern, arrange the pieces carefully on the bag fabric.

Position the dresses and scallops first. Iron in place. Repeat with arms and heads. Make sure the arms, hearts and scallops will meet when the side seam is sewn. Position the hearts so that the yellow side of the heart faces a blue dress and the blue side faces a yellow dress and press them. Cindy has hand-buttonholed around each of the appliqué shapes in a coordinating colour, and using one strand of embroidery thread.

When the appliqué is complete, and following the manufacturer directions, iron the fusible batting to the wrong side of the bag. Pin the bag/batting piece to the lining, right sides out. There will be an extra inch of lining fabric at one side edge of the bag, but don't cut it off.

Cindy has machine-quilted in the ditch around all the appliqué pieces using cotton thread.

MATERIALS

- 90cm (1yd) striped fabric for the bag, handles and tab (see note)
- 70cm ($\frac{3}{4}$yd) blue print for the base, scallops, handles, tab and bindings
- 50cm ($\frac{1}{2}$yd) yellow print fabric for the lining
- 20cm (8in) squares of three blue prints and three yellow prints for the dresses and hearts
- 5cm (2in) squares, six blue and six yellow for the arms
- 5cm (2in) squares of six tan prints for the heads
- 45cm (18in) fusible batting
- 30cm x 90cm (12in x 36in) fusible web
- Fusible interfacing
- Heavyweight interfacing
- 4cm ($1\frac{1}{2}$in) wooden button
- Lead pencil
- Scissors
- Embroidery thread to coordinate chosen fabrics
- Sewing machine
- Thread for machine-quilting
- Rotary cutter, ruler and mat
- Pressing equipment
- General sewing supplies
- 12mm ($\frac{1}{2}$in) flat button (optional)

FINISHED SIZE OF BAG

27cm ($10\frac{1}{2}$in) height

80cm ($31\frac{1}{2}$in) top circumference

NOTE:
- If using fabric without a stripe, only 50cm ($\frac{5}{8}$yd) is required. Seam allowances of $\frac{1}{4}$in are used throughout the bag construction and have been included in all the cutting instructions.
- It is recommended fabrics be 100 per cent cotton, pre-washed and ironed. Fabric and batting requirements are based on materials 112cm (44in) wide.
- Fusible batting will give your bag more body than normal batting. If this is unavailable use ordinary batting but iron a piece of lightweight fusible interfacing to the wrong side of your bag after the appliqué has been completed.

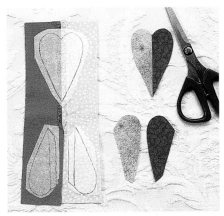

Photograph 1. *Centre the middle of the fusible-web heart over the seamline.*

BASE OF BAG

❖

Iron the fusible batting to the wrong side of the base fabric. Pin-baste the batting and lining together, right sides out. Machine-quilt the base in a grid of vertical and horizontal lines 1½in apart.

Trace the base pattern from the pattern sheet onto a piece of tracing paper or heavyweight interfacing, remembering to place it on the fold where indicated. Pin it to the quilted base fabric and carefully cut it out.

BAG ASSEMBLY

❖

Fold the bag, right sides together, and stitch the side seam, carefully matching hands, hearts and scallops. Fold the extra inch of lining fabric over the seam, turn the raw edge under and Slip-stitch it in place to cover the seam.

With the right side of the bag facing out, pin-mark the bag and the base into quarters. Pin the bag to the base, wrong sides together, aligning the pin-marks. Baste if desired.

Using the 2½in binding strip cut one end at a 45-degree angle. Press under a ¼in hem. Fold the strip in half, length-wise, wrong sides together and press. Place the binding strip on top of the bag piece matching the raw edges with those of the bag and base.

Cindy recommends removing the tray table from the sewing machine, for ease of stitching the bag together. Carefully stitch the binding, bag and base together overlapping the ends of the binding. Where the binding overlaps, Slip-stitch the join together and trim off any excess.

Fold the binding over the raw edge and Slip-stitch it to the base.

HANDLES

❖

For the six handle pieces, press under ¼in on one long edge of each handle strip and lay it on a flat surface with the right side facing down. Place a strip of batting, adhesive side up on the wrong side of the handles. Fold the raw edge over the batting about ½in then fold over the finished edge to the cover raw edge and press it. Slip stitch it in place.

Layer a blue, a stripe and a blue handle piece and pin them together. Plait evenly and firmly. Pin the ends to hold them. Repeat to make a second handle.

Spread the ends of the plait slightly and stitch across to secure them using photograph 2 as a guide. Pin the handles to the right side of the bag 3in from either side of centre, aligning the raw edges of the handle with the raw edge of the top of the bag. Stitch them to the inside of the bag using a ⅛in seam allowance.

TAB

❖

Using the three 1in x 18in strips, fold the raw edges of the long sides to meet in the centre and press. Then fold the strip in half lengthwise, and press it. Plait the three strips together in the same manner as for the handles. Make a loop in the centre of the plait large enough to fit over your button. Slip-stitch the plait together where it crosses over and pin the ends to the centre of the right side of the bag, raw edges together and stitch. Make another binding strip in the same manner as the bottom one. Pin it to the right side of the bag, overlapping the ends, and stitch it. Fold the binding to the inside and Slip-stitch it to the lining. Cindy added a ½in button under the large wooden button so the edge of the tab can slip under. ❁

Photograph 2. *Spread the ends of the plait slightly and stitch across them to secure.*

Tropicana

*Using the popular Snowball block, Carolyn Swart has used a collection of
brilliant orange and purple prints in this bright quilt.*

CUTTING

❖

From the 8in squares of scrap fabrics, cut:
- 110, 7in squares, making sure the grainline runs straight, for the background blocks.

From the 7in squares of scrap fabric, cut:
- 110, 6in squares for the appliqué circles.

From the 7in squares of dark scrap fabric, cut:
- 22, 6in squares for border circles.

From the border print fabric, cut:
- five, 7in strips. Crosscut into 22, 7in squares for the border blocks
- seven, 2½in strips for binding.

PREPARATION

❖

With the compass and sharp lead pencil, trace a 5¾in and a 5in circle onto thin cardboard. Cut them out carefully on the line and use them to make plastic templates. Use the 5¾in template and lead pencil to trace two circles onto freezer paper and cut them out. With the lead pencil, trace around the 5in template as many times as the thin sheet of cardboard will allow. Spray-starch and iron all the background appliqué blocks. Fold them in half, twice and press. With a ruler and blue water-erasable pen, draw lines along these folds. Spray-starch and iron all the fabric scraps for the circles and iron a freezer-paper circle onto two of them. Place four squares under the freezer-paper block and cut it out around the freezer-paper circle. Remove the freezer-paper circle and repeat this method again until you have the required number of circles for your quilt. With a long length of thread, leaving a 4in tail, sew a small running stitch around each circle, ¼in from the raw edge. Place a cardboard circle on the wrong side of the

MATERIALS

- 20.5cm (8in) squares of assorted scrap fabrics for the background – a total of 110 is required
- 18cm (7in) squares of assorted scrap fabrics for the appliquéd circles – a total of 110 is required
- 1.5m (1⅝yd) print fabric for border background blocks and binding
- 20cm (6in) squares of assorted scrap fabric in darker shades for border half-circles – a total of 22 is required
- 3.7m (4yd) backing fabric
- 178cm x 193cm (70in x 76in) wool batting
- Rotary cutter, ruler and mat
- Template plastic
- Freezer paper to draw two, 5¾in circles
- Compass
- Sharp lead pencil and sharpener
- Fine tip black marker
- Blue water-erasable pen
- Large sheet of thin cardboard
- Large and small scissors
- Basting pins
- Appliqué pins
- Appliqué needles
- Machine needles (12/80)
- Sewing machine with drop feed dogs
- Quarter inch foot, darning foot, quilting foot
- Variety of coloured threads to match the appliqué circles, neutral thread for piecing and the bobbin, coordinating coloured thread for machine-quilting, monofilament thread
- Spray starch
- Iron

FINISHED BLOCK SIZE

15cm (6in)

FINISHED QUILT SIZE

167cm x 184cm (66½in x 72½in)

NOTE: It is recommended that fabrics be 100 per cent cotton, pre-washed and ironed. Requirements are based on fabric 112cm (44in) wide. This quilt is made by hand-appliquéing circles onto squares, cutting into quarters and machine-piecing into blocks. Carolyn suggests reading all the instructions before commencing the quilt. The blue wash-out pen is permanent if not rinsed in cold water prior to pressing.

fabric and draw up the thread. Smooth out the gathers and securely knot the ends of the thread. Spray-starch and press the circle with the cardboard still inside. Once cooled, remove the cardboard.

APPLIQUE

❖

Lay the circles onto the background squares. Lay out a dozen or so squares at a time and mix and match the circles over the blocks to give a pleasing colour selection. Fold the fabric circle in half twice and finger-press to give the centre, making sure the grainline is straight. Open out and place a pin at the centre or

Photograph 1. *Appliqué the circle to the centre of a background square.*

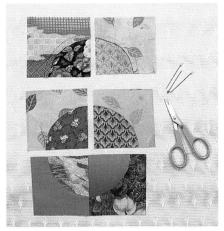

Photograph 2. *Trim away the background leaving a ¹/₄in seam.*

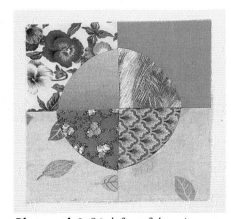

Photograph 3. *Stitch four of the units together to make a completed block.*

Photograph 4. *Stitch the border units into pairs adding a single unit for each of the corners.*

mark a dot with the blue pen. Pin the centre of the circle to the centre of the background block matching the fold lines. Pin all around the circle and with thread to match the piece being appliquéd, Slip-stitch it in place as shown in photograph 1. Gently press the block and use the rotary cutter to cut the block into quarters along the blue lines. With small sharp appliqué scissors, snip away the background fabric from the appliqué leaving a ¹/₄in allowance from the stitching line as shown in photograph 2.

BLOCK CONSTRUCTION

❖

Four of the quarters are joined to make one block. Carolyn had no set colour plan when piecing her blocks. Using photograph 3 as a guide, randomly select four quarters for each block and place in piles for quick machine-piecing. Attach the ¹/₄in foot to the sewing machine and thread the top with a coordinating colour. Stitch the quarter-block sections together into a block of four, making sure the centre seam is pinned and abutted in opposite directions. Make a total of 110 blocks and press them lightly.

BORDER CONSTRUCTION

❖

Centre a dark circle on a background block and appliqué it in place. Press the block and cut it into quarters, snipping away the background fabric. Put aside four of the quarters for the corners. Join the remaining quarters in pairs and press them. Make 42 half-blocks.

Join a quarter to one end of four of these units to make the corner sections as shown in photograph 4.

QUILT ASSEMBLY

❖

Lay out the blocks in 10 rows across and 11 down. Place a half-block at the end of each row and at the top and bottom. Place a single quarter in each corner. Pin and join a border section to each end block, then join the 10 blocks into a row making sure all seams are aligned.

Join the rows together and press the quilt top gently.

BACKING

❖

Cut the length of the backing fabric in half and remove the selvedges. Join the two pieces together and press the seam open.

QUILTING

❖

Layer the backing fabric wrong side up, batting and the quilt top right side up and baste. The featured quilt has been machine-quilted diagonally across each block in both directions and all the rows of blocks were ditch-quilted.

BINDING

❖

Join the strips with a bias seam and press them open. Fold the binding in half and then with raw edges even, join the binding to the front of quilt, mitring the corners as you go.

Trim the backing and batting leaving a scant ¹/₄in beyond the quilt top. Roll the folded edge to the back of quilt and slip-stitch it in place.

Label and date your quilt. ✲

Four-pointed Scrappy Star

Jennie Burton has written the instructions for this delightful quilt which dates from the 1930s and provides a wonderful opportunity to use those scraps which are too small for most projects

TEMPLATES

❖

The two templates A and B are finished size and seam allowances of ¼in must be added when cutting the pieces from the fabrics. Using a fine-tipped permanent marking pen, trace the templates onto template plastic and cut them out.

Identify each template and mark with the grainline. If machine-piecing is preferred, add seam allowances to the templates.

CUTTING

❖

The featured quilt has been constructed in a charming but somewhat haphazard fashion and there are discrepancies in the number of pieces in various rows.

To simplify construction and make the quilt symmetrical, the pieces have been arranged into 33 rows with the odd-numbered rows beginning and ending with an octagon and the even-numbered rows beginning and ending with a star. The size of the quilt could be increased or decreased according to your needs.

To cut the pieces from the fabrics, noting the grainline, place the templates on the wrong side of the fabrics and trace around them with a sharp pencil. This is the sewing line.

Place a quilter's quarter ruler on the sewing lines and rule in the ¼in seam allowance. Cut out the pieces.

From the fabric for the background, cut:

– 413 octagons, template A.

A total of 412 stars are required and each star is made from four template B pieces. In the featured quilt the opposite points of the stars are made from the same fabric.

From the variety of scrap fabrics, cut:

– 1648 pieces, template B.

CONSTRUCTION

❖

To make each star, following photograph 1, join four star points into two sets of two points along one short side. Join the two sets together to form a star, matching the seams at the intersection.

The stars are joined, as shown in photograph 2, alternately with the octagons to form the quilt top. To join the pieces, stitch along one side of the star, pivot at the centre and stitch to the next point.

Make 17 rows beginning and ending with an octagon from 13 octagons and 12 stars and 16 rows beginning and ending with a star from 13 stars and 12 octagons.

When all 33 rows have been made, join the rows together pivoting the stitching at the points of the octagons and the seams joining the star points. The odd-numbered rows begin and end with an octagon and the even-numbered rows with a star. When the rows have been joined, trim the seams slightly and press the quilt top well.

The edges of the featured quilt have been trimmed to create straight edges around the finished quilt. Alternatively, the edges of the pieces could be left untrimmed and the binding added by pivoting around the angles.

To straighten the edges of the quilt top, place it on a flat surface and trim evenly around the edge so the joins between the star points are at the edge of the quilt top. Use of a rotary cutter, quilter's ruler and mat would simplify this task.

BACKING

❖

Cut the length of backing fabric in half, remove the selvedges and join the two lengths together to make a backing a

MATERIALS

- 5m (5½yd) of quilter's muslin for the background
- A wide variety of assorted scrap fabrics. Small scraps are suitable as two star points can be cut from a 7.5cm (3in) square
- 4.8m (5¼yd) of backing fabric
- 60cm (⅔yd) or 1m (1⅛yd) of binding fabric (optional: see instructions for the binding)
- Single-bed sized batt. Jennie recommends fine wool batting for hand-quilting
- Neutral-coloured cotton thread for piecing
- Cotton quilting thread
- Template plastic
- Pencil
- Fine-point permanent marking pen
- Quilter's quarter ruler
- Rotary cutter, quilter's ruler and mat (optional)

FINISHED QUILT SIZE

170cm x 224cm (67in x 88in)

NOTE: It is suggested fabrics be 100 per cent cotton, pre-washed and ironed. Material requirements are based on fabric 112cm (44in) wide. A seam allowance of ¼in is used throughout the project for either hand or machine-piecing. It is recommended that the seam allowances be trimmed when the piecing has been completed to lessen bulk for quilting.

Photograph 1. *To make each star, join four star points into two sets of two points along one short side. Join the two sets together to form a star, matching the seams at the intersection.*

little larger than the quilt top with one vertical join. Press the seam open.

Before basting the layers of the quilt together, carefully press both the quilt top and the backing. Tack the layers together, making sure they are wrinkle-free.

The layers can be tacked together using a square grid with each line of stitching about 6in apart.

QUILTING

The featured quilt has been hand-quilted in a simple square pattern, which ignores the pieced design. The design of the quilt presents many possibilities for fine quilting. A motif could be quilted in each octagon and the stars quilted in the ditch or an all-over design such as the Baptist Fan pattern of concentric part circles would be suitable.

BINDING

Turning the backing fabric to the front of the quilt and hand-stitching in place has finished the featured quilt. Alternatively, the edge of the quilt could be finished with a conventional binding.

If the edge of the quilt is to be left untrimmed; a bias binding will fit the angles of the edge more easily than a straight binding.

Wrapped Edge
To finish the quilt in this manner trim the excess backing fabric leaving approximately 1¼in beyond the edge of the quilt top and trim the batting even with the edge of the quilt top. Fold the backing to the front of the quilt, turn the raw edge under and hand-stitch in place.

Convential Binding
Made from eight, 2½in strips cut from the full width of the fabric, joined with bias seams. Press the seams open and fold the binding lengthwise, wrong sides together and press it. Aligning all raw edges, stitch the binding to the quilt using a ¼in seam allowance, mitring the corners as you go. Roll the binding to the back of the quilt and stitch it in place.

Bias Binding
Make the binding from a 36in square of fabric using the continuous method as shown on page 94, cutting the strips 2½in wide. Trim the excess batting and backing even with the edge of the quilt top.

Fold the binding lengthwise, wrong sides together and press it. Pin the binding to the front of the quilt with the raw edges of the quilt and the binding even, creating a small tuck at each peak and valley.

If machine-stitching the binding, sew from pin to pin, removing each pin when the machine needle is in place.

Turn the folded edge of the binding to the back of the quilt and hand-stitch it in place, taking a small tuck at each valley and treating the peaks in a similar way to mitred corners.

Sign and date your quilt, as it is tomorrow's heirloom! ❊

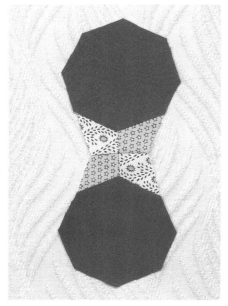

Photograph 2. *To make the rows, join the stars alternately with the octagons by stitching along one side of the star, pivoting at the centre and stitching to the next point.*

Jennie Burton has an extensive stock of antique and vintage quilts and tops, as well as old and antique sewing tools. She can be contacted at 7 Vincent Street, Balmain NSW 2041, phone (02) 9818 1346, fax (02) 9818 5694. Email jennifer_burton@hotmail.com

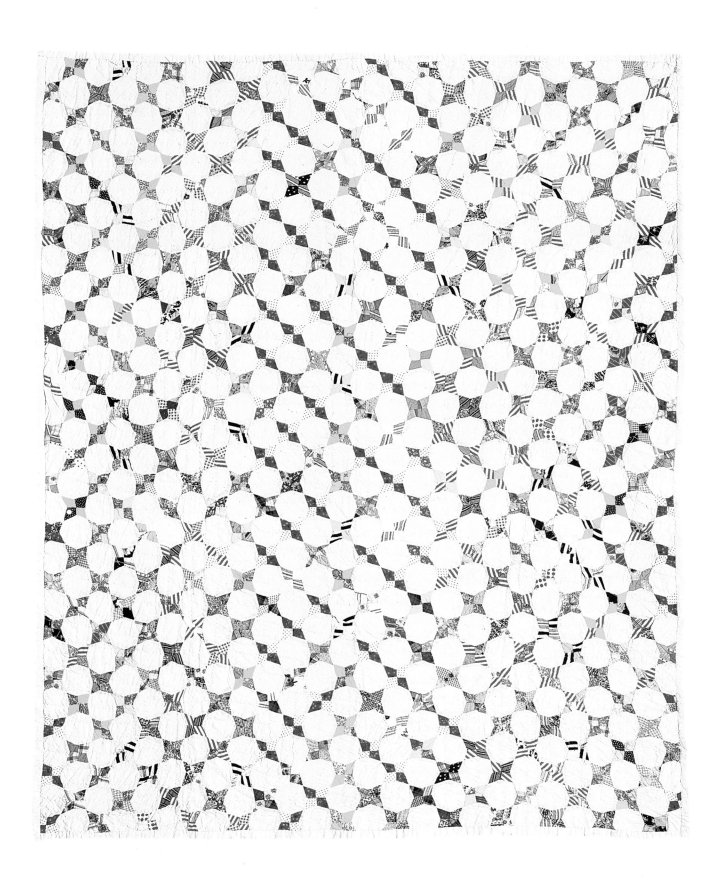

Six Degrees of Separation

Nola Archer made this quilt as part of a challenge with instructions to use every fabric in the Jennifer Sampou Designer Essentials range – and adding only one other fabric.

TEMPLATES

❖

Templates A-D are cutting size with ¼in seam allowances included. Template E for the appliqué diamonds, is finished size. However, for some of the diamonds it has been used as cutting size.

PREPARATION

❖

Templates A-E are printed on the pattern sheet. Trace them onto template plastic and identify each one, ensuring grainlines are clearly marked. Cut them out on the line.

CUTTING

❖

From the background fabric, cut:
– one, 120in length for the backing
– eight, 6½in strips for the borders
– 16, template D for the setting triangles
– 72, template A for the centre triangles.
From the medium fabrics, cut:
– 72 sets of three template B for the bars.
From the bright fabrics, cut:
– 72 sets of three template C for the star points.
From the light fabrics, cut:
– 20 template E for the appliquéd diamonds.
From the binding fabrics, cut:
– 13, 1¾in x 20in strips for the binding.

BLOCK CONSTRUCTION

❖

A total of 72 triangle blocks is required. Pin-mark the centre of one side of triangle A and the shorter side of template B.

Matching the pin-markings, pin and sew them as shown in diagram 1, pressing the seam towards the template B piece.

Lay a template C diamond along the right-hand end of the second template B bar, offsetting the ends to ensure the edges will meet when the diamond is opened out, as shown in diagram 2. Then pin and stitch them. Sew a diamond to each end of the third bar, as shown in the diagram, pressing all seams towards the bar.

Using diagram 2 as a guide, pin-mark the centre of the bars and the centre triangle. Stitch, matching the pin-marking.

QUILT ASSEMBLY

❖

The quilt is constructed in eight rows of nine triangles. The triangles point up or down alternately.

Using the photograph of the quilt as a guide, lay out your triangles. Nola arranged the triangles with red bars in a gentle curve from top right to lower left and the other colours in a colourwash arrangement in the corners.

Pin an upward-pointing triangle to the downward triangle next to it, right sides together and matching seamlines and centre marks. Sew them carefully and press seams open. Repeat until you have 32 pairs of up and down triangles.

Pin an upward-pointing triangle to the down triangle in a pair, matching seam lines. Sew them into a unit of three triangles in a row and press the seams open. Make seven more of these units.

Sew a unit of three to a pair of triangles, matching seamlines and pressing the seams open. Sew two more pairs to this strip, ensuring the strip begins and ends with an upward-pointing triangle. Stitch a triangle D to each end of your strip, to make the ends square. Sew the remaining blocks into rows as above, matching the layout in the photograph,

MATERIALS

• 5.7m (6¼yd) solid black for the background, border and the backing

• Assorted medium and bright scraps to total 2.4m (2¾yd). Nola used two packs of 7in charm squares from the Jennifer Sampou Designer Essentials range.

• 20cm (8in) light fabrics for the appliqué diamonds

• 25cm (10in) each of five bright fabrics for the binding

• 150cm x 200cm (60in x 76in) cotton batting

• Template plastic

• Permanent marking pen

• Pencil

• Sewing machine

• Black thread for the piecing

• Appliqué needle

• Light thread for the appliqué

• Round toothpick

• Freezer paper

• Rotary cutter, ruler and mat

• 30cm (12in) square of felt for the quilting template (optional)

• Quilting thread: red, black

• Chalk pencil for marking the quilt

• Walking foot for machine-quilting

FINISHED BLOCK SIZE

20cm (8in) equilateral triangle

FINISHED QUILT SIZE

133cm x 174cm (52½in x 68½in)

NOTE: It is recommended that fabric be 100 per cent cotton, pre-washed and ironed. Requirements are based on fabric 112cm (44in) wide. All cutting measurements include a ¼in seam allowance.

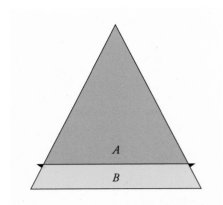

Diagram 1. Matching the pin-markings, pin and sew.

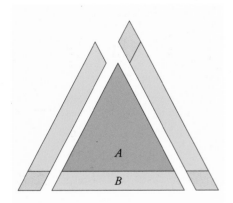

Diagram 2. Triangle assembly diagram.

and pressing the seams open. Join the rows carefully, matching points and intersecting seams.

BORDERS

❖

Join the eight 6½in strips into four sets of two strips. Trim two strips to 56½in and pin-mark them into quarters. Pin-mark the sides of the quilt into quarters and, with right sides together and matching the pin-markings, pin the borders to the quilt sides. Stitch and press the seam towards the border. Trim the other two strips to 52½in and in the same manner, add these to the top and bottom of the quilt. Stitch and press towards the border.

APPLIQUÉ

❖

Trace around template E onto the dull side of the freezer paper, cut out the shapes and mark the grainlines. Iron them to the right side of the diamonds so that the seam allowance protrudes on all

sides. Using the quilt photograph as a guide, appliqué them in place using matching thread. Use the toothpick as you stitch, to roll the fabric edge under, level with the edge of the freezer paper.

BACKING

❖

Cut the backing fabric in half, remove the selvedges and join them together with one horizontal seam. Layer the backing, batting and the quilt top and baste.

QUILTING

❖

Nola machine-quilted in red circles inside the hexagons, and in black circles in the border. The stars have been ditch-quilted in red and she also drew around template E to make diamonds at the edges of the unfinished stars and quilted them in black. Nola used a 10½in felt circle as her quilting template. Using the quilting diagram as a guide, pin the circle to the central star of six triangle units and machine-quilt around them using a walking foot, without stitching into the felt.

BINDING

❖

Join the strips with 45-degree seams and press open. Fold it in half lengthwise, wrong sides together and press it. Beginning halfway along one side, stitch it to the front of the quilt using a ¼in seam, and mitring the corners. Adjust the binding length, open it out and join the ends with a 45-degree seam. With wrong sides together again, finish stitching. Turn it to the back and hand-stitch it in place. ❈

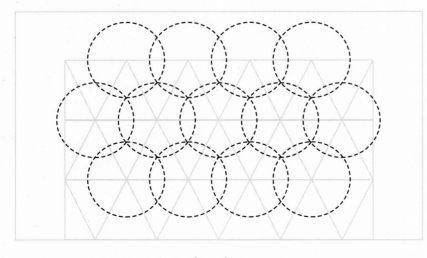

Quilting diagram

Dazzling
Delights

Scrappy Daffy

This cosy quilt – made from a variety of flannel scraps – is by Joanne Knott and it's sure to keep you as snug as a bug in a rug.

CUTTING

❖

This quilt consists of 42 Square-in-a-Square blocks separated by sashing strips. For each block, from the assorted scraps, cut:

– one, 2in x 8in strip from a light and a dark fabric for the four-patch units

– two, 3½in squares from a contrasting fabric for the four-patch squares

– two, 5⅛in squares from a light fabric, cut each once on the diagonal, to form the four background triangles.

From the light flannel print, cut:

– 56, 3in squares for the sashing squares.

From the dark green sashing fabric, cut:

– 97, 3in x 9in strips.

From the border fabric, cut:

– nine, 8in strips.

From the binding fabric, cut:

– ten, 3in strips.

BLOCK CONSTRUCTION

❖

A total of 42 Square-in-a-Square blocks is required for this quilt. For each block, sew together two, 2in x 8in rectangles lengthwise. Crosscut these at 2in intervals to yield four pairs. Following photograph 1, stitch two of these units together to form a Four Patch, ensuring you alternate the colours. Sew a 3½in contrasting square to each of these units. Stitch these units together to form the centre square of the block.

Using photograph 2 as a guide, stitch a light triangle along each edge of the completed unit to form the Square-in-a-Square block.

QUILT ASSEMBLY

❖

The quilt is constructed in seven rows each with six blocks which are separated by sashing strips.

Using the quilt layout diagram as a guide and beginning and ending with a sashing rectangle, alternate the blocks with the sashing rectangles.

Make eight sashing strips, starting and ending with a sashing square and alternating sashing rectangles with sashing squares.

Stitch the strips together, in rows as shown in the quilt layout diagram to make up the centre of the quilt.

MATERIALS

- Large assortment of flannel fabric scraps minimum size 9cm (3½in) square for the blocks
- 1.9m (2⅛yd) dark green flannel for the sashing
- 60cm (⅔yd) light flannel print for the sashing squares
- 2.5m (2¾yd) medium flannel print for the border
- 90cm (1yd) solid green for the binding
- 5.5m (6yd) backing fabric
- 227cm x 254cm (90in x 100in) batting
- Rotary cutter, ruler and mat
- Sewing machine
- Piecing thread
- Machine-quilting thread
- Scissors
- General sewing supplies

FINISHED BLOCK SIZE

21.5cm (8½in)

FINISHED QUILT SIZE

215cm x 242.5cm (84½in x 95½in)

NOTE: It is recommended that fabric be 100 per cent cotton, pre-washed and ironed. Requirements are based on fabric 112cm (44in) wide.

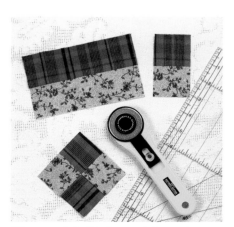

Photograph 1. *Stitch two of these units together to form a four-patch, ensuring you alternate the colours.*

Photograph 2. *Stitch a light triangle along each edge of the completed unit to form the Square-in-a-Square block.*

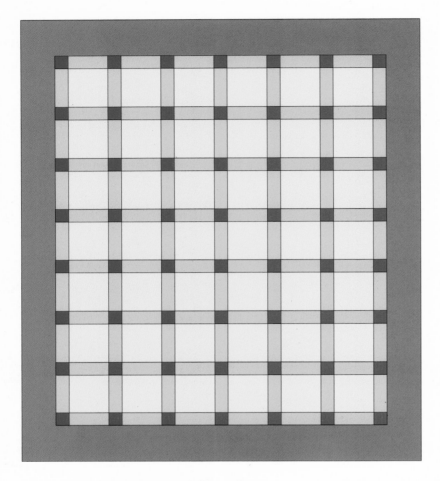

Quilt layout diagram

Pin-mark the top and bottom of the quilt top and the border strips into quarters. Stitch the borders to the quilt top, once again making sure that you match the pin-markings.

BACKING

❖

Cut the backing fabric into two equal lengths, remove the selvedges and join the two pieces to make a backing a little larger than the quilt top with one seam which is pressed open.

Layer the backing, batting and quilt top, making sure you smooth out each layer. Pin or hand-baste the layers together in a grid pattern.

QUILTING

❖

Joanne has machine-quilted her quilt using a tan coloured thread to cross-hatch the centre of each block. She has added a swirly design in the corner triangles of the blocks as well as in the sashing and the borders.

BORDERS

❖

Stitch the 8in border strips together into one long length. Measure across the centre of the quilt lengthwise, it should measure 79$\frac{1}{2}$in from raw edge to raw edge. Trim two border strips to equal this measurement.

Pin-mark the opposite sides of the quilt top and the border strips in quarters. Carefully stitch the borders to the quilt top, making sure that you match the pin-markings.

Measure across the centre of the quilt widthwise, it should measure 83$\frac{1}{2}$in from raw edge to raw edge. Trim two border strips to this measurement.

BINDING

❖

Stitch the binding strips end to end using 45-degree seams and press the seams open. Then press the binding wrong sides together, and carefully sew it in place using a $\frac{1}{4}$in seam, mitring the corners as you go.

Trim the edges of the batting and backing to $\frac{1}{2}$in from the stitching line. Fold the binding to the back of the quilt and neatly hand-stitch it in place.

Sign and date your quilt. ❋

PREPARATION

❖

Trace the finished-size pattern pieces onto template plastic, marking the grainline.

Cut them out on the line, then place the template back over the pattern piece and trace around it to ensure that it is accurate.

Lay the template right side up on the wrong side of the fabric, and trace around the template with a lead pencil leaving a ¼in seam allowance around each piece.

CUTTING

❖

From the orange print fabric, cut:
– two, template A
– four, template F.

From the purple print fabric, cut:
– two, template A
– four, template F.

From the assorted green print fabrics, cut:
– three, template C
– three, template E.

From the assorted beige print fabrics, cut:
– four, template B
– four, template D.

From the almond beige border fabric, cut:
– four, template E.

From the green binding fabric, cut:
– three, 1½in bias strips for the cushion piping
– one, template C
– one, template E.

From the cushion backing fabric, cut:
– two, 11in x 18in rectangles.

BLOCK ASSEMBLY

❖

Lay out the pattern pieces using the cushion layout as a guide.

Following photograph 1, pin and stitch pieces C and D together. Stitch this section to piece A, then stitch B to the opposite end as shown in photograph 2. Stitch a total of four units together in the same manner.

Using photograph 3 as a guide, pin and stitch two units together to form half the block. Make up the second half of the block in the same manner, pin and stitch the two halves together.

Photograph 4 shows the completed block measuring 10½in, raw edge to raw edge.

Pin and stitch the length of each green piece E to each beige E to create the four borders for the block.

Pin and stitch a border unit to the opposite sides of the block. Stitch each of

Photograph 1. *Pin and stitch C and D together.*

Photograph 2. *Stitch this section to A, then stitch B to the opposite end.*

MATERIALS

- 20cm (¼yd) of three assorted green fabrics for the pieced block
- 30cm (12in) square each of orange print, purple tone-on-tone and three assorted almond beiges for the pieced block
- 30cm (12in) square of green for the cushion border
- 30cm (12in) square of almond beige print for the cushion border
- Fat quarter of green for the piping, and the pieced block
- 50cm (20in) square of batting
- 50cm (20in) quilter's muslin for the lining
- 4 buttons
- 2m (80in) of piping cord
- Fat quarter of coordinating fabric for the cushion back
- 41cm (16in) cushion insert
- Template plastic
- Neutral thread for piecing
- Quilting thread
- Pencil
- General sewing supplies
- Sewing machine for cushion construction (optional)

FINISHED CUSHION SIZE

42cm (16½in) square

NOTE: It is recommended that fabrics be 100 per cent cotton, pre washed and ironed. Material requirements are based on fabric 112cm (44in) wide.

Photograph 3. Pin and stitch the two units together to form half the block.

Photograph 4. The completed block measuring 10¹/₂in, raw edge to raw edge.

the orange F pieces along the diagonal to a purple F. Sew these units to either end of the pieced border units using the photograph of the cushion as a guide. Pin and stitch these units to the top and bottom cushion block – it should now measure 15¹/₂in raw edge to raw edge – and press it gently.

PIPING

❖

Using a 45-degree seam join the bias strips together to create one continuous length of bias. With the right side out, fold the length of bias over the piping cord. Stitch close to the piping either by hand, or by machine using a zipper foot.

Pin the piping to the front of the cushion, lining up the raw edges and easing it around the corners.

Leaving some piping hanging free at each end, stitch it in place by hand or again using the zipper foot, then trim the cord only to fit exactly.

Slip-stitch the piping ends to join them, then overlap the piping casing neatly and stitch it.

QUILTING

❖

Layer the lining, batting and cushion front right side up and baste them together in a grid pattern. Janette has outline-quilted each of the block pieces ¹/₄in from the seam.

The triangles in the borders have been quilted diagonally, connecting the seams in the border units.

CUSHION ASSEMBLY

❖

Trim the batting and backing to the edge of the cushion top.

Fold and press a ¹/₄in hem on one long side of each of the cushion backing pieces. Fold over another 1in, press and then stitch.

Lay one side on top of the other with the folded edges overlapping in the centre. Stitch four evenly spaced buttonholes in the hemmed edge of the top piece to fit your buttons. Again lay the two pieces flat with the top edge overlapping the bottom piece. Stitch across the overlapping edges at the top and bottom.

Measure across the cushion back and trim it to 16in.

With the right sides facing, pin the cushion front and back together and stitch through all layers.

Trim the corners and turn it to the right side. Sew four buttons on the under side of the cushion back in alignment with the buttonholes. Place the cushion insert inside it and fasten the buttons over it. ❈

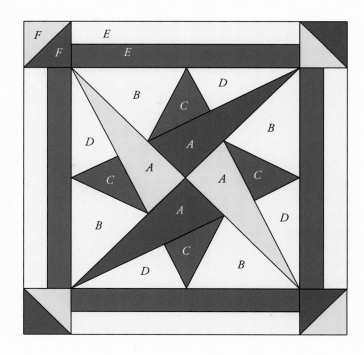

Happy Hearts

*A Nine Patch block with appliquéd hearts was Jacky Hens' choice
for her quilt when she received blocks from the Cotton Reel Quilters'
friendship swap on her birthday.*

PREPARATION

❖

The pattern for the heart appliqué is printed on the pattern sheet. Trace the shapes onto template plastic or transfer to lightweight cardboard with a fine-tipped marking pen or a sharp pencil. Mark the grainline and cut out the templates accurately keeping the edges smooth and even.

The quilt has 18 appliquéd heart blocks. Trace around each heart template 18 times on freezer paper, then cut out the shapes on the line.

CUTTING

❖

Using the freezer paper templates, place the curves of the hearts on the bias grain of the fabric and adding 1/4in seam allowances, from the scrap fabric for the hearts, cut:

– 18 large hearts
– 18 small hearts.

From the scrap fabric for the squares, cut:

– 157, 3 1/4in squares, 85 squares are for the Nine Patch blocks and 72 squares are for the corners of the appliquéd heart blocks.

From the full width of the background fabric, cut:

– five, 9in strips and crosscut the strips into 18, 9in squares for the background of the appliquéd blocks. These squares are cut slightly larger than required to allow for any distortion which may occur during the appliqué process
– seven, 3 1/4in strips and crosscut the strips into 68, 3 1/4in squares for the Nine Patch blocks.

From the full width of the fabric for the first border and the quilt binding fabric, cut:

– five, 1 1/2in strips for the first border
– seven, 3in strips for the binding.

From the full width of the fabric for second border, cut:

– seven, 6 1/2in strips.

APPLIQUE BLOCKS

❖

Fold the 9in squares for the background of the appliqué blocks in half twice and mark the centres to assist with placement of the appliqué.

Prepare the hearts for appliqué by placing the shiny side of the freezer paper on the wrong side of the fabric and pressing lightly. Turn the seam allowance over the edge of the freezer paper and finger-press it in place, using spray starch where necessary to obtain a crisp edge. Baste in place.

To make each block, following photograph 1 and using a small blind stitch, appliqué the small heart in place on top of the large heart using matching or slightly darker thread than the heart being appliquéd.

Matching the centre point of the background square and the positioning cross on the large heart, pin or baste the hearts in place on the background. Appliqué the large heart. It is not necessary to stitch the area beneath the small heart, use this area to ease the freezer paper out from the wrong side of the large heart. Appliqué the remainder of the small heart, easing the freezer paper out before making the final stitches.

When all 18 blocks have been appliquéd, press and trim each block to a 8 3/4in square.

Draw a diagonal line across the wrong side of 72, 3 1/4in squares for the corners of the heart blocks. Following photograph 2, place one square, right sides together, at each corner of each

MATERIALS

• A wide variety of assorted scrap fabrics

- 157, 8.5cm (3 1/4in) squares are required for the Nine Patch blocks and the corners of the heart blocks

- 36, 15.5cm (6in) squares or fabric scraps for the appliquéd hearts

• 1.8m (2yd) of background fabric

• 90cm (1yd) of fabric for the first border and the quilt binding

• 1.3m (1 3/8yd) of fabric for the second border

• 3.2m (3 1/2yd) of backing fabric

• 153cm x 204cm (60in x 80in) batting

• Freezer paper for appliqué (optional)

• Template plastic or lightweight cardboard

• Cotton threads to match fabrics for appliqué

• Neutral-coloured thread for piecing

• Quilting thread

• Pencil

• Fine-tipped permanent marking pen

• Rotary cutter, quilter's ruler and mat

• Can of spray starch.

FINISHED BLOCK SIZE

21cm (8 1/4in)

FINISHED BLOCK SIZE

142cm x 184cm (55 3/4in x 72 1/4in)

NOTE:
• It is recommended fabrics be 100 per cent cotton, pre-washed and ironed.
Material requirements are based on fabric 112cm (44in) wide.

• Jacky's quilt was appliquéd by hand, machine-pieced and quilted. If preferred, the quilt could be made completely by hand or machine.

• Seam allowances of 1/4in are included in cutting requirements for the pieced sections of the quilt but should be added when cutting the appliqué pieces.

Photograph 1. Appliqué the small heart in place on top of the large heart using matching or slightly darker thread than the heart being appliquéd.

Photograph 2. Place one square, right sides together, at each corner of the block and stitch along the line. Turn the inner triangle created by the line of stitching back to the corner of the block and trim the centre layer leaving a 1/4in seam allowance.

block and stitch along the drawn line. Turn the inner triangle created by the line of stitching back to the corner of the block and check that it matches the outer edges of the block background. Trim the centre layer leaving a 1/4in seam allowance and press.

NINE PATCH BLOCKS

❖

To make each of the 17 Nine Patch blocks required for the quilt, and following photograph 3, arrange four, 3 1/4in squares of background fabric and five, 3 1/4in squares of scrap fabric into three rows of three squares. Stitch the squares in each row together and press the seams towards the scrap fabrics. Join the rows together, abutting the seams together at the intersections and press. Each block should measure 8 3/4in including seam allowances.

ASSEMBLY

❖

Following the quilt construction diagram, arrange the blocks into seven rows of five blocks, alternating the appliquéd blocks with the Nine Patch blocks. If possible, use a design wall or floor, rearranging the blocks until there is a pleasing distribution of colour.

Stitch the rows of blocks together and press the seams towards the Nine Patch blocks. Join the rows together to form the centre of the quilt top, abutting the seams together at the intersections. Press.

FIRST BORDER

Measure the length of the quilt through the centre and, using the five, 1 1/2in strips cut for the first border, make borders to fit the two sides of the quilt. Pin mark the sides of the quilt top and the border

Quilt layout diagram

Photograph 3. *Arrange four squares of background fabric and five squares of scrap fabric into three rows of three squares.*

than the quilt with one horizontal join. Press the seam open. Layer the quilt top, the batting and the backing and baste or pin the three layers together.

QUILTING

❖

Jacky's quilt has been machine-quilted. She quilted in the ditch around the Nine Patch blocks, the corners of the appliquéd blocks and the first border. The appliquéd hearts were outline-quilted and each square of background fabric in the Nine Patch blocks was quilted across each diagonal. The background of the appliquéd blocks and outer triangle, created by the diagonal lines of quilting at the centre of each side of the Nine Patch blocks, were stipple-quilted.

BINDING

❖

Join the seven, 3in strips cut for the quilt binding into one long length with bias seams and press the seams open. Press the length of binding in half with wrong sides together. Trim the excess batting and backing even with the edge of the quilt top. Beginning approximately halfway along one side, stitch the binding to the edge of the quilt with a ¹/₄in seam, mitring each corner. Turn the folded edge of the binding to the back of the quilt and hand-stitch it in place.

Jacky added a label made from two appliquéd hearts to the back of her quilt. Each of the participants in her friendship group signed the label. ❋

Jacky Hens conducts patchwork and quilting classes and workshops. She can be contacted by telephone on (02) 4739 4175.

strips into quarters and join the borders to the quilt top matching the pins. Press the seams towards the borders.

Measure the width of the quilt top through the centre and use the remaining strips to add borders to the top and bottom of the quilt top in the same manner as the side borders.

SECOND BORDER

Use the seven, 6¹/₂in strips cut for the second border to add the second border to the quilt top in the same manner as the first border.

BACKING

❖

Cut the length of backing fabric in half, remove the selvedges and join the two pieces to make a backing a little larger

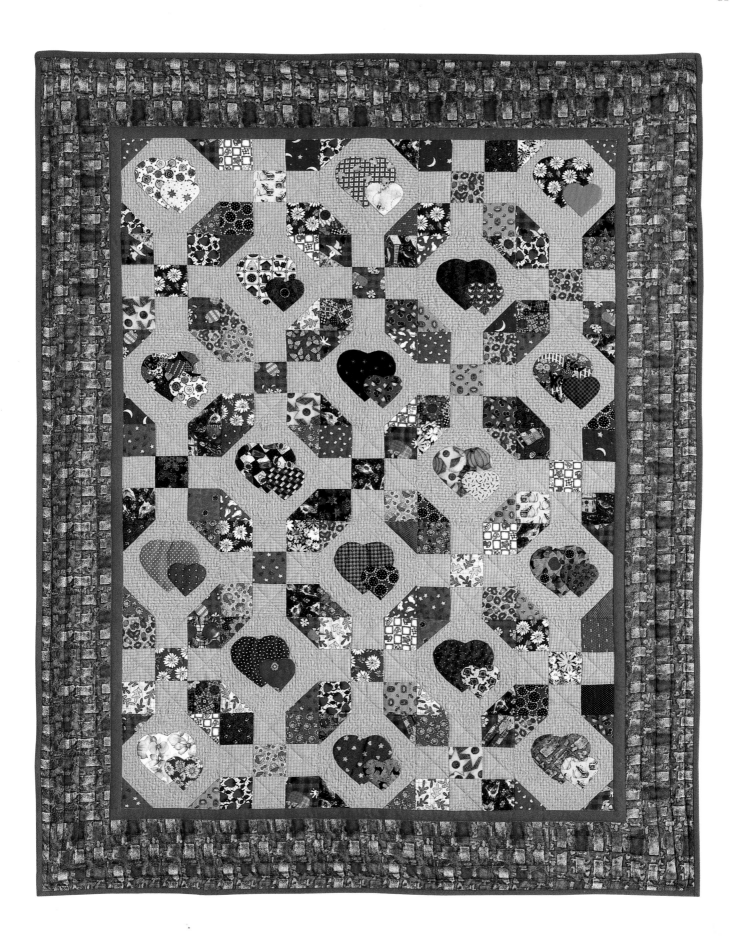

Bush Beauty

Karen Stone's quilts inspired Kay Fernihough to make this quilt which features the New York Beauty block in bright colours and a background fabric with an Aboriginal design.

PREPARATION

❖

Using the patterns provided on the pattern sheet, accurately trace the finished-sized templates A, B, C, D and E onto the template plastic and carefully cut them out on the line. Identify each template and mark with the grainline. Templates A and E are used in reverse.

To cut the pieces, place the fabric right side down and, using a sharp pencil, trace around the templates placing a dot at each corner. This is the sewing line. Mark a line $\frac{1}{4}$in out from this as the cutting line.

CUTTING

❖

From the first border fabric, cut:
– nine, $1\frac{1}{2}$in strips.
From the length of the multicoloured print fabric, cut:

– two, $5\frac{1}{2}$in x 94in strips for the second border
– two, $5\frac{1}{2}$in x 86in strips for the second border.

From the width of the multicoloured print fabric, cut:
– ten, $2\frac{1}{2}$in strips for the binding.
From the remaining multicoloured print fabric, cut:
– 80, template A
– 80, template AR.
For each block, cut:
– five, template C of 'peak' fabric.
– four, template B of 'valley' fabric
– one, template E of 'valley' fabric
– one, template ER of 'valley' fabric
– one, template D of 'base' fabric.

BLOCK CONSTRUCTION

❖

A total of 80 blocks is required. Using diagram 1 as a guide, stitch together pieces E, C, B and ER to form the arc in

MATERIALS

- 6m (6½yd) multicoloured large print for the background, second border and binding
- Assorted light, medium and dark scraps that read as solid colours, totalling 70cm (¾yd). Minimum size: 10cm (4in) square for base of fan
- Assorted light and dark scraps that read as solids for the 'valleys' of the fan totalling 4m (4½yd)
- Assorted bright toned scraps for the 'peaks' of the fan totalling 3.7m (4yds)
- 50cm (½yd) solid black for the first border
- 8.3m (9yds) backing fabric
- Queen-size batting
- Neutral-coloured thread for piecing
- Monofilament thread for quilting
- Multicolored metallic thread for quilting
- Template plastic
- Fine-tipped permanent marker
- Rotary cutter, ruler and mat
- Sewing machine

FINISHED BLOCK SIZE

24.5cm (9in) square

FINISHED QUILT SIZE

214cm x 260cm (84½in x 102½in)

NOTE: It is recommended that fabrics be 100 per cent cotton, pre-washed and ironed. Requirements are based on fabrics 112cm (44in) wide. All strips are cut across the width of the fabric unless otherwise stated.

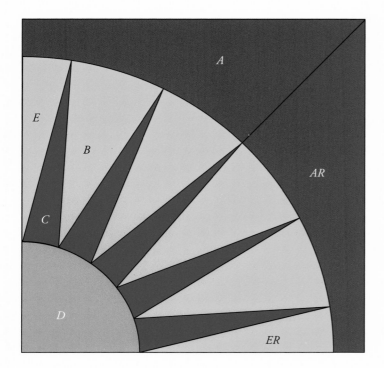

Diagram 1. *Block layout diagram.*

Diagram 2. *Lay the pieced arc right side up, centre the base and pin it.*

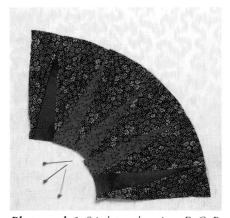

Photograph 1. *Stitch together pieces E, C, B and ER to form the arc.*

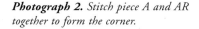

Photograph 2. *Stitch piece A and AR together to form the corner.*

the centre of the block as shown in photograph 1. Lightly press the seams in the same direction.

Place the pieced arc right side up on your work surface. Centre the base right side down on top of it, positioning it as shown in diagram 2. Pin them together at the centre. Pin at both ends of the curve, then place one pin between the centre and the outside pin on both sides.

With the base on top, carefully sew along the curve, making sure to keep the edges even as you sew. Lightly press the seam allowance towards the pieced arc.

Using photograph 2 as a guide, stitch piece A and AR together to form the corner of the block.

Referring to photograph 3, stitch the arc to this unit in the same manner as before.

ASSEMBLY

Following the quilt layout diagram, arrange the completed blocks into 10 rows of eight blocks each.

Experiment with the orientation of the blocks and the colour combinations until you are happy with the overall effect, as this quilt can be put together in a number of different ways to form different designs. Sew the blocks into rows and then sew the rows together. Press the quilt top.

FIRST BORDER

Sew the $1\frac{1}{2}$in border strips into pairs, cut the leftover strip in half and sew each to a joined strip. Measure through the centre of the quilt from top to bottom. It should measure $90\frac{1}{2}$in raw edge to raw edge. Cut the two longer strips to this measurement. Pin-mark the sides of the quilt top and the border strips into quarters. With right sides together stitch the strips to the quilt top, making sure that the pin-markings are matching.

Measure through the centre of the quilt from right to left. It should measure $74\frac{1}{2}$in raw edge to raw edge. Then cut the remaining two strips to this measurement. Pin-mark the top and bottom of the quilt top and border strips into quarters. Stitch the borders to the quilt top, again making sure that the pin-markings are matching.

SECOND BORDER

Stitch the second border strips into one long length. Measure through the centre of the quilt from top to bottom. It should measure $92\frac{1}{2}$in from raw edge to raw edge. Cut the two longer strips to equal

Quilt layout diagram

Photograph 3. *Stitch the arc to this unit in the same manner as before.*

backing fabric which is a little larger than the quilt top. You will have a backing which has two vertical seams. Press these seams open.

Layer the backing fabric, batting and quilt top, centring them as you go. Make sure that you carefully smooth out each layer and then pin or baste the three layers together.

QUILTING
❖

Kay has used Monofilament thread to ditch-quilt the peaks and borders, and to stipple-quilt the base of the block.

She used a variegated metallic thread to quilt between each peak, as well as at the point of the peaks and to the edge of each block. The metallic thread has also been used in the quilt's second border to continue the rays out from the blocks.

Kay recommends using the Monofilament and the metallic thread through the needle only, and to use cotton thread to match the backing fabric in the bobbin.

this measurement. Pin-mark the sides of the quilt top and border strips into quarters. Stitch the borders to the quilt top, making sure that the pin-markings are matching.

Measure through the centre of the quilt from right to left. It should measure 84½in raw edge to raw edge. Then again cut the remaining two strips to this measurement.

Pin-mark the top and bottom of the quilt top and border strips into quarters. Stitch the borders to the quilt top making sure the pin-markings are matching. Gently press the quilt top.

BINDING
❖

Trim the backing and the batting even with the edge of the quilt. Join the 2½in binding strips into one long strip using bias joins.

Press the seams open. Fold the strip in half wrong sides together and press it.

Starting at the bottom, sew the binding to the quilt using a ¼in seam allowance and mitring the corners as you go. Fold the binding to the back and carefully Slip-stitch it into place.

Label your quilt making sure that you include your name and the date.❈

BACKING
❖

Cut the backing fabric into three equal lengths and remove the selvedges. Join the length of the three pieces to make a

Cypress

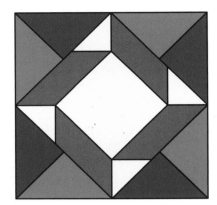

Premium Star

Rising Star

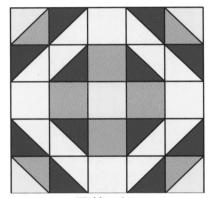

Wedding Ring

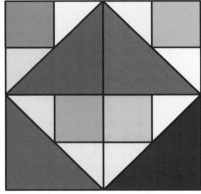

Arrow

Block Library

Understanding the system for dividing blocks into squares is essential when drafting quilting blocks. The ability to draft any block to any size opens many options to the quilter. If you can re-scale a pattern to suit your individual needs you will be free from the necessity of following patterns.

Before you start ruling lines, you need to understand the construction of blocks and learn to identify whether they are based on the Four Patch, Nine Patch, Five Patch or Seven Patch.

We all know the basic Four Patch block, which is effective in a chequerboard design. Arrow, Lantern and Pinwheel are other examples of simple Four Patch blocks. More complex

examples of Four Patches include Rising Star and Kansas Troubles.

The basic Nine Patch format is the foundation for blocks such as Jacob's Ladder and the more complex Wyoming Valley block.

Miller's Daughter is an example of a Five Patch, and Seven Patch blocks include Dove in the Window.

Dividing a square into a grid is the first step in drafting and, while it is a simple process, it should be done with great care as it is the basis of accurate templates. Start by drawing the outline of the block, using a fine-tipped pencil (if you are using a regular pencil you will need to sharpen it often) and ruler on a sheet of graph paper. Graph paper is not

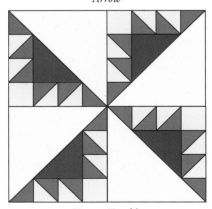

Kansas Troubles

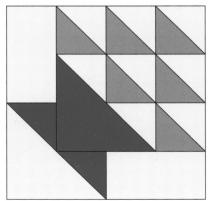

Flower Basket

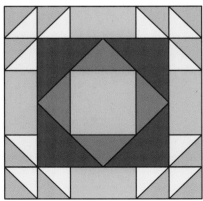

Double X

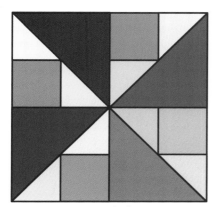

Pinwheel

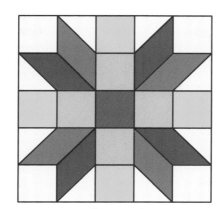

Miller's Daughter

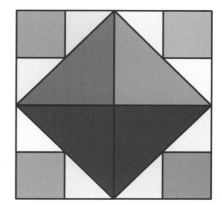

Box

always accurate, so use the grid only to determine right angles and as a guide for ruling straight lines. Use your ruler to measure the width and length of the block.

For complex blocks – those which are required to be drafted over a grid with more divisions than a basic Four Patch or Nine Patch – the following method is the easiest.

For example, to make an 8in Wyoming Valley block, a grid of six squares across and six squares down is required. Place the ruler over the block diagonally with the '0' on the lower left-hand corner. Pivot the ruler along the right-hand side of the block until a measurement which is easily divided by six aligns with the edge. In this case, 9in is the most appropriate as 9 divided by 6 is 1½in. Holding the ruler in this position, mark intervals of 1½in across the block. Rule lines through these five

points parallel to the right-hand side of the block. Turn the block 45 degrees and draw another five lines in the same manner. Check your grid to ensure it is accurate.

To experiment with drafting, use a tracing of this master grid. Align the ruler with as many intersections on the grid as possible when ruling in the design. Copy the completed design onto your master grid. Mark the block pieces to identify each template, any reversed pieces and grainlines. Your templates will be more accurate if they are traced off adjoining pieces.

Lastly, decide how the block will be pieced. The Wyoming Valley block is most easily pieced in nine units. Lay out the nine units in three rows of three, ensuring the correct rotation of each unit. Stitch the units together into rows, and then join the rows together carefully matching the intersections. ❋

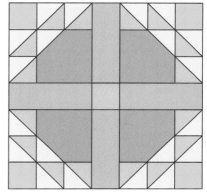

Dove in the Window

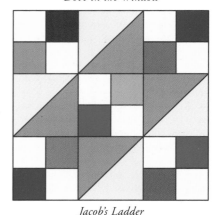

Jacob's Ladder

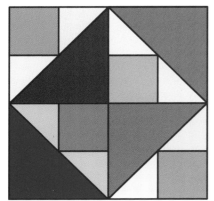

Lantern

Propeller

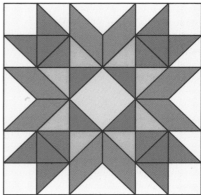

Wyoming Valley

Country
Scraps

Mini Butterflies

Dale Ritson was sent 25 butterfly cut-outs as a Christmas gift from an American pen friend. She supplied the rest, adding the butterfly-shaped border to continue the theme.

PREPARATION

❖

Using the permanent marking pen, trace the butterfly shape onto template plastic and cut it out, rechecking against the pattern for accuracy. Mark the grainline on the template. Trace 25 butterfly shapes onto the fusible webbing and cut out each one roughly.

CUTTING

❖

From the background fabric, cut:
- three, 4in strips and crosscut 25, 4in squares for the appliqué blocks
- four, 2½in strips for the outer border
- one, 16in square for the binding.
From the floral border fabric, cut:
- two, 1in strips and crosscut four, 1in x 19in strips.

APPLIQUE

❖

Press the fusible webbing to the wrong side of each of the butterfly fabrics and cut them out accurately on the line. Remove the paper backing from the butterfly shapes and, centring each butterfly on 4in background square, fuse them in place.

Using two strands of embroidery thread in either a matching or contrasting colour and following the diagram, stitch around the butterfly shape. Following the Stem-stitch diagram and with two strands of black embroidery thread, embroider the feelers and the body. Press each block from the wrong side.

Lay out the blocks in five rows of five. Then, when you're happy with the arrangement, stitch the blocks together using a ¼in seam. Pin the rows together ensuring that the block edges are aligned, then press them.

MATERIALS

- 25, 10cm (4in) squares assorted floral scraps for the butterflies
- 1.2m (1¼yd) background for butterfly blocks, border and binding
- 20cm (¼yd) floral fabric for the narrow border
- 80cm (32in) square of fabric for the backing
- 80cm (32in) square of thin batting
- Black embroidery thread for the centre and butterfly feelers
- Matching or contrasting embroidery thread for butterfly wings
- Thread for piecing and quilting
- 10cm (4in) fusible webbing
- Template plastic
- Permanent marking pen
- 2B pencil
- Rotary cutter, ruler and mat
- Sewing machine
- Basic sewing supplies
- Sandpaper-covered board
- Iron and ironing board

FINISHED BLOCK SIZE

9cm (3½in)

FINISHED QUILT SIZE

58.5cm (23in) square

NOTE: Material requirements are based on fabric 112cm (44in) wide. It is recommended fabric be 100per cent cotton, pre-washed and ironed. A ¼in seam allowance is used for the construction of the quilt and is included in the cutting instructions. The butterflies are Buttonhole-stitched in place — no seam allowance is required.

Photograph 1. *Centre each butterfly shape in place and Buttonhole-stitch around it.*

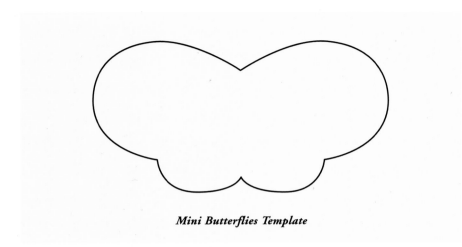

Mini Butterflies Template

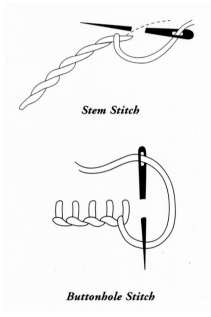

Stem Stitch

Buttonhole Stitch

BORDERS

❖

INNER BORDER

Pin-mark the centre of the top edge of the quilt and the inner border strip. Stitch the inner border to the quilt top aligning the pin-marking, starting and ending ¼in from the raw edge of the quilt top. Do not stitch into the seam allowance.

The border strip should extend beyond the quilt top on both sides to allow for mitring. Attach the three remaining inner border strips in the same manner. Lay the quilt top on the ironing board wrong side up and press the seam towards the border.

Carefully fold the border strip on a 45-degree angle, checking with a ruler to ensure that the outer edge forms a perfect right angle and press it gently. Stitch from the inner edge to the outer edge. Press the seam open and trim any excess fabric.

OUTER BORDER

Attach the outer solid border strips in the same manner as the inner border, then mitre the corners. Dale used the butterfly template and lead pencil to mark the shape of the quilt top's outer edge. Referring to the photograph of the quilt, line up the butterfly template and mark

the wing shapes with the 2B pencil, then carefully cut it out along the pencil line.

BACKING

❖

Iron the 80cm backing square and remove any selvedges.

Dale recommends that you pre-mark your quilt top before basting it. Using a 2B pencil, trace the butterfly shapes onto the quilt top in a pleasing pattern. Two quilting lines were used around each butterfly, spaced ⅛in apart.

QUILTING

❖

Layer the backing right side down, the batting and then the quilt top right side up. Ensure all layers are smooth and wrinkle-free, then baste the three layers together.

BINDING

❖

Trim the excess batting and backing even with edge of the quilt top. Using the continuous bias method from page 94, cut a continuous bias strip 1in wide and approximately 120in long.

Fold over a scant ¼in hem and press it gently. Using a single layer of binding only, pin the binding strip to the front of the quilt, right sides together and carefully sew the edges together with a scant ¼in seam, easing as you go.

Turn the folded edge of the binding to the back of the quilt and hand-stitch it in place using a matching thread.

Sign and date your quilt with a label using embroidery or a fine permanent pen. ✳

Photograph 3. *Add rounds of purple strips to the flower.*

Turn the purple strip back and press it flat. Trim the excess fabric at each end of the strip as indicated by the broken lines on the strip in the photograph.

Continue in this manner, stitching, folding and trimming, until all sides of the flower centre have been covered.

Add another three or four rounds of purple strips to the flower, as shown in photograph 4, ensuring the purple strips reach one edge of the foundation, which will become the lower edge of the flower to be joined to the stem.

Complete the block by adding the light green background strips in the same way.

STEMS AND LEAVES

To make the lower section of each of the flower blocks, from the dark green fabric, cut a stem and two leaf shapes.

To create added visual interest to each block, you can vary the size and shape of these pieces, however the stems must be cut 8in long. Using photograph 5 as a guide, place the stem at the centre of one, 8in square of interfacing, right side up and pin it in place.

From the light green fabrics, cut a strip which is 8in long and place it, right sides together over the stem. Then using a $^1/_4$in seam, stitch the strip to the stem making sure to stitch through all three layers. Turn the green strip back and press it flat.

Add another light green strip to the other side of the stem in the same manner. Fill the remaining area of the foundation with strips of the light green fabric.

Using your preferred method of appliqué and the patterns from the pattern sheet, add two leaves to each side of the stems.

Bev has used a machine Buttonhole Stitch to appliqué the leaves in place.

Photograph 4. Complete the block by adding light green background strips.

BLOCK ASSEMBLY

❖

Following photograph 5, carefully join the top and bottom sections of the block so the stem sits beneath the purple edge of the flower.

Trim the completed flower blocks to 8in x 15in which also includes the ¼in seam allowances.

QUILT ASSEMBLY

❖

Using the photograph of the quilt as a guide, arrange the blocks into five rows of six blocks with the flower blocks stepped down the quilt.

Once you are pleased with your arrangement, join the blocks together into rows and then join the rows together to form the centre of the quilt top.

FIRST BORDER

Measure the width of the quilt through the centre and, using the seven, 2in yellow strips, make borders to fit the top and bottom of the quilt. Pin-mark the edges of the quilt top and the border strips into quarters and join the borders to the quilt top, making sure that the pin-markings are matching. Press the seams towards the borders.

Measure the length of the quilt top through the centre and use the remaining strips to add borders to the two sides of the quilt top, in the same manner as the top and bottom borders.

SECOND BORDER

Corner Flowers

Using the four, 7in squares of interfacing, make flower blocks for the four corners of the second border in the same manner as the other flowers with yellow, purple and light green fabrics.

Photograph 5, opposite page. Join the top and bottom sections of the flower block so the stems sit beneath the purple edge of the flower.

CUBIC PUZZLER

© Susan Murphy
Embroidery Design

VALORI'S FLOWER

© Bev Darby

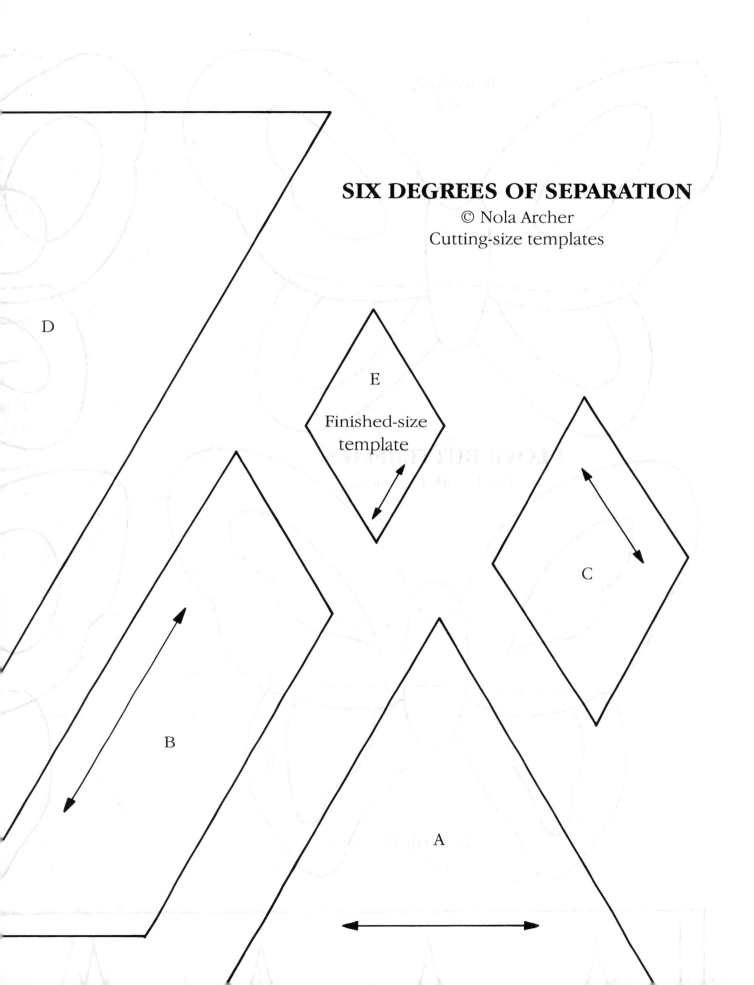

SIX DEGREES OF SEPARATION
© Nola Archer
Cutting-size templates

D

E

Finished-size
template

C

B

A

As these flowers do not have stems the light green fabric should border the flower on all four sides.

Press the blocks and trim them to 6½in squares.

Pieced Strips

Join the 22, 2in strips of purple fabric cut for the second border, along the long edges, into two sets of 11 strips, and then carefully press all the seams in the same direction.

Crosscut the sets of strips into 6½in sections and then join them to make four strips for the second border of the quilt. The top and bottom borders of the quilt each require 24 strips and the two side borders each require 38 strips.

Join the two side borders to the quilt top in the same way as the first border. Join one flower block to each end of the top and bottom borders and stitch these borders to the quilt top.

Press the quilt top.

BACKING

❖

Cut the length of backing fabric in half, cut one strip in half lengthwise and, with a wide seam, join one strip to each side of the full-width piece. Remove the selvedges and press the seams open.

Layer the backing fabric right side down, then the batting, and the quilt top right side up. Carefully smooth out each layer as you go. Then either pin-baste for machine-quilting or hand-baste in a grid for hand-quilting.

QUILTING

❖

Bev machine-quilted her quilt with Monofilament thread on the top of the

machine and cotton thread to match the backing fabric in the bobbin. She quilted in-the-ditch between the blocks, across the Log Cabin blocks, around the flowers and all the seams in the borders.

BINDING

❖

Trim the batting and backing fabric ¼in outside the edge of the quilt top.

Join the eight, 2½in strips cut for the binding with bias seams, press the seams open and press the length of binding in half, wrong sides together.

Beginning approximately halfway along one side and 8in from the end of the binding strip, stitch the binding to the quilt, ¼in from the edge of the quilt top, mitring at each corner. Stop stitching 4in before you reach the beginning and open out both ends of the binding. Then carefully join the two sides together with a 45-degree seam. Flatten the seam, refold the binding and finish sewing it to the quilt top. Turn the folded edge of the binding to the back of the quilt and hand-stitch it in place.

Add a label to your quilt with your name and the date you completed the quilt. You may also like to include where you recieved any of your fabric from, what type of fabric you used or how long it took to make the quilt. If the quilt is a to be a present for someone, include their name and a short message or poem to remind them of your friendship. ✳

Bev Darby teaches classes at A Little Patch of Country, 63 Princes Highway, Trafalgar Vic 3824. Telephone (03) 5633 2311.

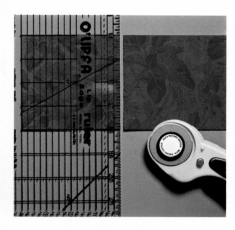

THREAD

There is a variety of threads for both machine and hand-sewing and when selecting threads consider the two pieces to be joined.

It is recommended that you use the best thread you can afford, matching the thread to the method of stitching and the type of fabric. For cotton fabrics, cotton thread is best, or cotton-covered polyester.

For piecing by hand or machine, select a colour that matches the darkest of the fabrics you are sewing. For stitching light and dark solid fabrics together, match the thread to the darkest fabric. To join two print fabrics, match the thread to a colour which is found in both fabrics. When stitching a print to a solid fabric, match the thread to the colour of the solid fabric.

If you are using a wide variety of fabrics, select a neutral-coloured thread such as grey or ecru that is a slightly darker shade that will blend in.

For appliqué, match the thread to the piece being appliquéd, or for overlapping appliqué pieces, the uppermost piece.

When machine-quilting, a cotton or decorative thread will show the stitches more prominently than a monofilament thread. Hand-quilting is best done using a specialised hand-quilting thread.

PINS

Glass-headed pins are very sharp (make sure you always take care when using them). This makes them ideal for piercing straight through fabric when you are lining up a seam or at a starting point.

Flower-headed pins are also very sharp and they are longer than normal sewing pins. The flattened heads allow them to lie close to the fabric, which is particularly useful for appliqué.

Appliqué pins are very short and fine.

Safety pins are used for holding quilts together for machine-quilting.

PENCILS

Pencils are used to mark sewing lines for hand-piecing and quilting designs. There are many quilting pencils available, from lead to chemical and specialised quilting markers. Whichever you use, test it first to make sure it washes out easily and read any manufacturer's instructions. The chemicals in some blue wash-out pencils may harm the fibres of some fabrics, so do not use them unless they wash out in cold water on a sample. Do not leave a marked quilt in the heat or stored away – always wash out the marker first. Quilting lines should only be marked once, as the second layer of markings will go straight through to the batting.

THIMBLES

A thimble is indispensable if you are quilting by hand. Some quiltmakers also like to use one on the finger underneath the work to push the needle back through the fabric. A special quilting thimble is available for those who like to quilt away from themselves using their thumb.

SCISSORS

You will need three pairs of scissors for patchwork. Sewing shears are used for cutting fabric only and they should be extremely sharp.

General household scissors are required for cutting paper, cardboard and template plastic, while small, sharp embroidery scissors are useful for clipping threads and seam allowances.

ROTARY CUTTER AND MAT

The rotary cutter is an excellent tool for cutting strips and a variety of geometric patchwork pieces, as well as creating straight fabric edges.

It also enables the accurate cutting of several layers of fabric at once. Select a cutter with a large blade and keep spare blades handy. Always cut on a self-healing mat especially designed for the rotary cutter. Extreme care must be taken when using and handling a rotary cutter – it is important to cut away from yourself and always retract the blade when it is not in use.

RULERS

A variety of rotary cutting rulers in imperial and metric measurements is available for cutting an assortment of shapes and strips. These rulers are well marked and sturdy.

A long ruler is the best for cutting border, binding and quick-piecing strips.

FRAMES AND HOOPS

A quilting frame or hoop is used to stop the layers shifting while you are hand-quilting. When quilting the edges of a quilt, it may be necessary to tack a handtowel to the edge so there is enough fabric to put into the hoop.

Choose a hoop with a diameter approximately the same measurement as the length from your elbow to your hand, so that you can reach to the far side of the hoop while you are quilting.

PREPARATION OF FABRICS

It is suggested that all fabrics are pre-washed and ironed before commencing the cutting of your quilt. This will not only pre-shrink the fabrics – so they do not shrink once in the quilt – but this also removes any excess dye and any stiffening sizing, ensuring that fabrics are much easier to handle.

Pre-wash coloured fabrics separately to avoid dyes staining other fabrics and always rinse them well – until the water runs clear.

Don't over-dry fabrics, as they may become very creased – iron them while they are still slightly damp. For creases which are hard to remove, spray them lightly with a mixture of $2/3$ water and $1/3$ vinegar.

If you are using the same fabric in both borders and block pieces, trim the selvedge and cut the borders first.

Position the templates on the fabric so that the arrows match the straight of grain. Mark a small arrow in the seam allowance indicating the straight-of-grain direction to ensure you don't place a bias edge on the outside of a block.

CHOOSING FABRICS

There are thousands of different fabrics available for quilters and when you first go fabric shopping, it helps to have an idea in mind about the predominant colour you require for your project.

One-way designs should always be considered carefully, as they need to be cut and pieced in one way and this is time-consuming.

Start by selecting either your favourite or your feature fabric first, then pull out fabrics that tone in with this fabric or complement it.

Complementary colours are opposite each other on the colour wheel – for example, green and red.

You could try a split-complementary arrangement by choosing the colours on either side of the opposite colour, such as red, yellow and blue.

Analogous colours are those that are next to each other on the colour wheel. Reds, oranges and yellows are all warm colours while greens, blues and purples are cool colours.

Triad colours are an equal distance apart on the colour wheel. That is, every fourth colour on the wheel – for example, blue, red and yellow.

Monochromatic colours are all the shades and tints through one colour, for example pink, lolly pink, red and deep ruby.

Polychromatic colour schemes use all the colours around the wheel, such as yellow, green, blue, red and orange.

TEMPLATES

A template is the pattern piece. Templates can be made of cardboard, old X-ray film, plastic such as the lid from an ice-cream container, or store-bought template plastic.

The edges of cardboard templates tend to wear with frequent use and must be replaced to ensure accuracy. It is important for templates used for hand-piecing and appliqué to be cut to the exact size without seam allowances, as they mark the stitching line – not the cutting line. For machine-sewing, include a $1/4$in seam allowance around all edges before cutting the template.

When marking templates, hold your pencil at a 45-degree angle to your ruler. Cut templates out exactly on the line, as cutting on the outside of the line will increase the size of the template.

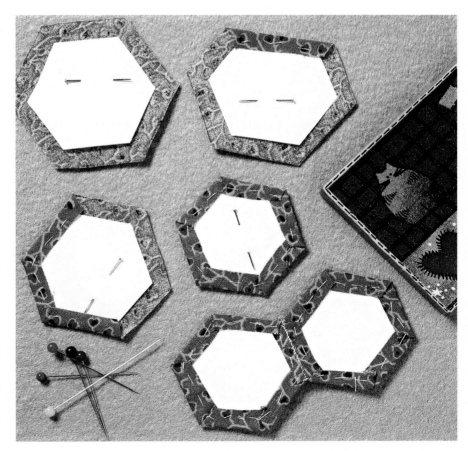

Once you have cut out the template, place it back down over the paper pattern piece and draw around it. If the lines are not exact compared to the original, remake the template.

HAND-PIECING

Pieces for hand-piecing require precisely marked seamlines – marked cutting lines are optional. To mark patches, place the template face down on the wrong side of the fabric and draw around it accurately with a sharp pencil. Leave space between patches for a $1/4$in seam allowance on all sides, which is added when they are cut out. It is sufficient to 'eyeball' the seam rather than measuring it. The pieces will be joined right sides together, so the seamline that is also marked on the wrong side of the fabric will be visible on both sides of the patchwork when sewing.

Knot the end of the thread and starting from the intersecting point, take a small stitch, then Backstitch to anchor the seam. Stitch along the seamline using running stitch, making sure it aligns with the pencil lines on both pieces. Take a small Backstitch again every two or three stitches. Sew to the intersecting point and then Backstitch to finish.

Finger-press the seam towards the darker fabric. As you stitch your next seam, ensure that the seam allowances remain free and are not stitched through. When the block is complete, press it with a dry iron from the wrong side and then press it from the front.

MACHINE-PIECING

Sewing-machine manufacturers have now designed $1/4$in feet to make sewing the perfect seam easier.

When using these feet, the edge of the fabric should be aligned with the edge of the foot. The distance from the needle to the edge of the foot is $1/4$in.

Chain-piecing is a great saver of thread and time. After stitching a pair of patches together, leave them under the foot and feed the next pair in. This will create a chain of stitches between the pairs. When all the pairs are sewn, snip them apart.

ROTARY OR TEMPLATE-FREE CUTTING

It is important to use the rotary cutter accurately and efficiently to ensure straight pieces. Make sure your rotary cutting mat is on a firm, flat surface. Before cutting strips, you must create a straight edge on the fabric. Fold the fabric in half lengthwise with the selvedges together, making sure they are aligned properly and with the right side of the fabric facing out. Place it on the cutting board and, aligning one of the cross lines on the rotary cutting ruler with the fold of the fabric, trim the edge. Carefully rotate the cutting board to avoid disturbing the alignment of the fabric layers and cut the required strips.

Squares, rectangles and triangles can all be cut from strips. When cutting squares and rectangles, remember to add $1/2$in to the finished measurement required. For a 2in finished square cut a $2^1/2$in square. For a 2in x 4in finished rectangle, cut $2^1/2$in x $4^1/2$in. Remove any selvedges after cutting a strip and before crosscutting.

Half-square triangles are half a square with the short sides on the straight of grain and the long side on the bias. To cut these triangles, cut a square $7/8$in larger than the finished short side of the triangle for seam allowances.

For quarter-square triangles, start with a square which is 1¹/₄in larger than the finished long side of the triangle. The short sides of quarter-square triangles are on the bias and the long sides are on the straight of grain. Cut the squares on the diagonal twice and trim the points off the corners of the seam allowances for a neater finish.

ENGLISH PAPER-PIECING METHOD

❖

This hand-piecing technique involves basting fabric over thin cardboard or paper templates. The shapes are stitched together to form blocks and ultimately to form a quilt. Although time-consuming, this method results in sharp, precise seams and a professional finish. It has the added advantage it can be put down and picked up again at will, and also carried around.

When hand-piecing over paper, cut out an exact-sized lightweight cardboard template for every piece in the quilt. Cut out the fabric shape using the cardboard pattern and also include a ¹/₄in seam allowance all around.

Place the cardboard template in the centre of the wrong side of the fabric shape and, working one side at a time, fold the seam allowance over the template.

Ensure the corners are folded in neatly before basting the seams. For easy removal of the basting, start with a knot on the top and finish with a simple double stitch.

To join the patches together, place them right sides facing and with the corners aligned. Using a matching thread and starting ¹/₄in from the corner, join the edges required with Whip Stitch. Stitch to the end of the seam, then turn the piece and Whip-stitch back to the point where you started. Turn the work again and again stitch back to the starting point to create a secure double seam. Make sure you do not stitch through the cardboard template and keep your stitches fairly small – they should not be visible from the right side of the fabric. Make each block separately by sewing the smallest pieces together first to form units. Join smaller units to form larger ones until the block is complete. Press the blocks, then join them together to form rows and join the rows to form the quilt top.

When all the pieces are joined together, turn the quilt over, press it well with a warm iron and allow it to cool. Carefully remove the basting stitches and lift out the templates.

JOINING BLOCKS

❖

Blocks joined edge to edge
Join the blocks to form strips the width of the quilt. Pin each seam very carefully by inserting a pin wherever the seams meet, at right angles to the seam. Press all seam allowances in the odd-numbered rows in one direction and all seam allowances in even-numbered rows in the opposite direction.

When all the rows are complete, pin two rows together so that the seamlines match perfectly. Join the rows in groups of two, then four, and so on, until the top

much. Pin the pieces to the background fabric from the back to avoid threads becoming entangled on the pin. Ensure that the placement of the pieces remains correct as you stitch and baste them before stitching if necessary.

Cut a length of thread, approximately the same length as your forearm, and make a small knot in one end of it. Make sure the knot sits underneath the piece being appliquéd, then bring the thread from the back through the background fabric and catch a couple of threads on the appliqué piece. When you begin to appliqué, make sure the needle enters the background fabric directly opposite where it came out on the top piece and slightly under the piece being appliquéd.

When you have completed the stitching, finish off on the wrong side of the work with a couple of small Backstitches. Do not leave pins in your work for too long in a humid climate.

is complete. Press all the seam allowances in one direction, either up or down.

Blocks joined with horizontal and vertical sashing

Join the blocks into strips with a vertical sash between each pair of blocks. Pin-mark the top and bottom of the horizontal sashing strips at suitable reference points, such as block and sashing intersections, before joining them to the block rows.

Then pin-baste the horizontal strips in place, aligning the reference points, and stitch them.

PRESSING

Press the seam allowances to one side, usually towards the darker fabric. Press quilt blocks flat and square making sure there are no puckers.

To correct any problems in blocks, sashing strips or borders, remove a few stitches to ease the puckers and re-sew to secure it.

APPLIQUE

Appliqué is not a difficult technique but basic rules do apply. Curves should be smooth, points should be sharp, and there should be no puckers. Begin by marking around the template onto the right side of the fabric. Cut out the shape with a $1/4$in seam allowance. Turn the seam allowance under and baste it. For sharp curves, sew a tiny running stitch just to the outside of the marked line and gather it slightly so the curve sits evenly. For sharp points, mitre the corner as you are basting, and cut away any excess fabric, but take care not to cut away too

BORDERS

Selecting the fabrics and border designs for a quilt is very important. The correct border fabric should enhance the colours and the design of a quilt. Striped fabrics work wonderfully as they can be mitred to create quite a dramatic frame around a pieced centre.

For some other quilt designs, the background on the quilt may be extended to become the border. This will create the illusion that the pieced work is floating on the background.

Extra dimension can be added to a border by using more than one fabric. Joining different fabrics together at random until the required length of your borders is reached is one way to create a superb visual texture.

The first step in adding a border to a quilt is to measure the quilt top through its centre to determine its width and length. Pin-mark borders and the edges of the quilt into quarters and match the pins as you join the pieces.

To make mitred corners, working on the wrong side of the quilt top, smooth one border over the adjoining one and draw a 45-degree diagonal line from the inner seam line to the point where the outer edges of the two borders cross. Turn them over (the bottom one is now on top), and draw a diagonal line from the inner seam line to the point where the outer edges cross.

Align the pencil lines with the right sides together, and join them. Cut away the excess fabric and press the seams open. Repeat the process for the other corners of the quilt.

BATTING

Batting – or wadding as it is sometimes called – is the middle layer in a quilt 'sandwich'. Battings made from natural and synthetic fibres are available both in packs and by the metre.

The thinner battings are easier to machine-quilt as there is less bulk to move around, while thicker battings are ideal for tied quilts.

Natural-fibre battings – and especially cotton – tend to cling to the fabric of a quilt, so it is much more stable and won't move around as much when you are pinning or quilting.

The batting should always be at least 5cm (2in) larger than the quilt top when it is basted as the quilting stitch will draw it up slightly.

When purchasing batting, it is very important to read all the washing instructions before you make your final choice. Some battings may require pre-washing or they may not be suitable for frequent laundering.

BACKING

Make the quilt backing about 2in larger than the quilt top on each side. This can involve sewing lengths of fabric together to create the width required for larger quilts. Join them, stitching with a $1/2$in seam allowance, remove the selvedges and press the seam allowances either open or to one side.

MARKING FOR QUILTING

It is best to mark quilting designs before you begin basting and there are many techniques for doing this. The design may either be placed under the quilt top or on top of it, and can be transferred in a variety of ways.

Mark the design lightly on the quilt top using a hard lead pencil and make sure to mark all the dark-coloured fabrics with a chalk pencil.

When water-soluble pens are used, it's advisable to test the marker of your choice on a sample to make sure it can be easily removed.

Some quilting can be done without having to mark the quilt top at all. Outline-quilting $1/4$in from the seam around the patches or quilting in the ditch (quilting right next to the seam on the side without the seam allowances) can be done by 'marking' the quilting line by eye.

Other straight lines may also be marked as you quilt by using a piece of masking tape that is pulled away after a line is quilted along the edge.

Remove all masking tape when not actually quilting and be sure not to leave a marked quilt in the sunlight.

LAYERING THE QUILT

Place the backing, wrong side up, on a flat surface. Then spread the batting over the backing, making sure that they both stay smooth and even. Next, place the quilt top, right side up, on top of the batting. Baste it with safety pins about a fist-width apart for machine-quilting, or thread-baste it for hand-quilting.

Pin the layers to secure them while you are thread-basting and thread a needle without cutting the thread off the reel. Beginning in the centre of the quilt top, make large stitches from the centre diagonally out to the corner and finish with a Backstitch. Then cut the thread from the reel leaving enough thread to stitch to the opposite corner. Thread the needle and continue basting. Repeat this on the opposite diagonal, creating an 'X'

shape across the quilt. Then baste rows 4in and 6in apart, again working from the centre outwards, and stitching vertical lines in diagonally opposite quarters and in horizontal lines on the alternating quarters. Baste around the edges of the quilt. Do not put your hands under the quilt while you are basting, as the layers will not remain even.

HAND-QUILTING

Quilting is done in a short running stitch with a single strand of thread that goes through all three layers. Use a short Betweens needle, beginning with a No 10 and progressing to a No 12 Betweens as you gain confidence. Using a thread approximately 18in long, start by taking a

long stitch of about 1in through the top and batting only, coming up where the quilting will begin. Tug on the thread to pull the knotted end through the quilt top and secure it within the batting. Then make straight, even stitches that are the same size on the top and bottom of the quilt. To achieve tiny stitches, push the needle with a thimble on your middle finger while you guide the fabric in front of the needle with the thumb of one hand above the quilt, and with the thumb and index finger of the other hand below the quilt.

To end a line of quilting, make a knot in the thread about half a needle length from the fabric. Stitch back through the hole the needle last came out of and travel the needle through the batting (across the quilt) until the knot disappears through the quilt top. Bring the needle up about 2in from the entry point, pull it taut and snip the thread – the end of the thread should also disappear into the quilt.

To continue the same row of quilting, knot the thread and insert the needle approximately 1in away from your last stitching hole. Bring the needle up through that hole and stitch in the same manner as before. When you have completed the quilting, carefully pull out the basting threads.

MACHINE-QUILTING

To quilt by machine successfully, you require a walking foot that is compatible with your sewing machine. A walking foot works like feed dogs for the upper fabrics to feed the quilt thickness through the machine evenly.

It is also important to stitch with a sharp needle, preferably a jeans needle, as blunt needles tend to push the batting through the backing fabric.

Needles should be changed regularly to avoid problems. A normal sewing thread can be used in both the needle and the bobbin. When using normal threads you need to be more accurate with your quilting stitch as it shows up more on the finished quilt.

Mistakes are much easier to hide with monofilament thread, which is a very fine, clear nylon thread that blends with all colours. This thread is available in a smoke-colour ideal for working on dark fabrics. When working with monofilament thread, a normal thread should still be used in the bobbin.

Machine-quilting is a skill that takes time to perfect, so be patient.

BINDING

Binding is the fabric that encases the raw edges of the three layers in the quilt. For extra durability it is usually doubled, except on some miniature quilts. Unless the binding is to be used on a curved edge, it can be cut on the straight of grain.

Cut sufficient $2^{1}/_{4}$in strips selvedge to selvedge to go around the quilt top. Join the strips together using 45-degree seams and press the seams open. Cut one end to a 45-degree angle. Press the binding in half lengthwise with the wrong sides together and then press under a single

hem on one end of the binding strip. Using a $^{1}/_{4}$in seam allowance and starting about 6in from the pressed hem, stitch the binding strip to the quilt top edge, stopping $^{1}/_{4}$in from each corner.

Remove the quilt from your machine and fold the binding strip at 45 degrees towards the top of the quilt. Then fold the binding strip down level with the next side of the quilt to create a neat corner. This will make a mitred corner when the binding is folded to the back of the quilt. Continue stitching, starting at the top edge of the folded strip. Repeat the process for all the other corners.

Stop stitching approximately 12in from the starting point with the needle in the fabric and, with the quilt remaining

under the machine, insert the end of the strip inside the other end, trimming off any excess. Finish stitching the binding strip on, then turn the folded edge over to the back of the quilt and Slip-stitch it in place. Slip-stitch the overlap of the join and the mitred corners to secure them.

LABELS

It is important to sew a label onto the back of your quilt including your details, the date you completed the quilt and any other relevant information, such as who the quilt was made for. ✳

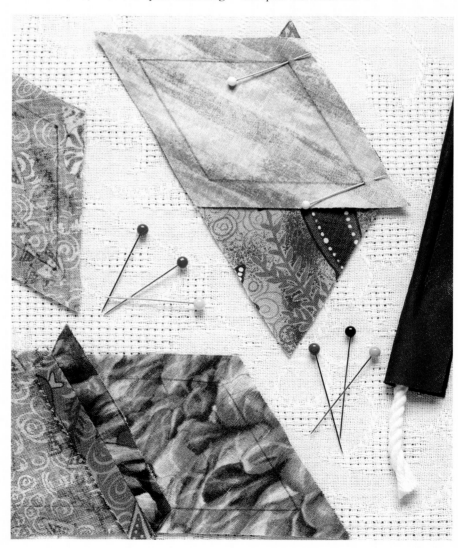

Continuous Bias Binding

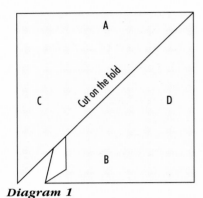

Diagram 1

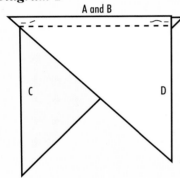

Diagram 2

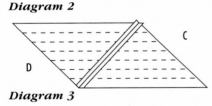

Diagram 3

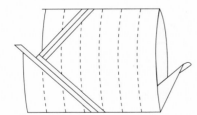

Diagram 4

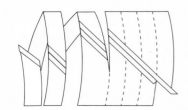

Diagram 5

Continuous bias binding is a useful method of cutting bias strips for binding a quilt or for appliqué stems.

It is made from a square of fabric on the straight grain, cut in half diagonally. The length and width of the bias needed determines the size of the square required. The square size should be evenly divisible by the required width of the binding. Refer to the step-by-step continuous bias diagrams.

With right sides together, pin and sew with a short machine stitch along the two short sides of the cut triangles with a ¼in seam. Press the seam open. This creates a parallelogram. Using a large ruler or dressmaker's square, mark the finished cut width on the wrong side of the fabric on the bias grain. Connect the marks with a straight line. With right sides together and dropping down one bias width, match the pencil markings and pin. There can sometimes be a small amount of fabric left when marking the cutting lines. Ignore this and continue to make the binding, then cut off this small amount when the bias is complete. Sew the unit together to form a tube, as shown in the diagrams. Begin cutting on the marked lines to form one long strip. This method allows an economical use of fabric and a true bias is achieved.

BIAS STRIP CALCULATIONS

To estimate the size of the square required for a given length of bias:

Multiply the length of the strip by the cut width of the strip to find the area. This will give you the size of the square needed to yield the required length.

To find the size, using a calculator, press the square root button (square root symbol) and round the number up.

For example, if your quilt requires approximately 300in of 2½in-wide binding, 300 x 2½ = 750. The √ of 750 is 27.4, so you will need a 28in square.

To estimate the length of bias that can be cut from a square:

Multiply the width of the square by the length of the square to find the area.

Divide the area of the square by the width of the binding strip to find the length of the strip that can be cut.

For example, if you have a 20in square to cut 2½in-wide binding, 2½in will divide into the square eight times.

Multiply 8 x 20in (one side of the square) to find this method will yield approximately 160in of binding. ✳

Continuous bias diagrams

1. Cut a square in half on the diagonal.
2. With right sides together, stitch A to B with a ¼in seam allowance. Overlap the points of A and B.
3. Press the seam open and mark lines the width of the required strip along the bias edge.
4. With right sides together and dropping down one bias width, match pencil markings, pin and sew to form a tube.
5. Cut along the marked lines to form one long strip.

Index

Published by
Craftworld Books
A division of Express Publications Pty Ltd, ACN 057 807 904
Under licence from EP Investments Pty Ltd, ACN 003 109 055 (1995)

2 Stanley Street
Silverwater NSW 2128
Australia

First published by Craftworld Books 2000

Publisher Sue Aiken
Photographic Director Robyn Wilson
Editor for Australian Patchwork & Quilting Lorraine Moran
Editor Lorinda Freeman
Production Editor Justyna Lupa
Editorial Assistant Clare Johnson
Project Editors Robyn Brookman, Lisa Moore
Technical Consultant Becky Peters
Subeditors Gabrielle Baxter, Keiasha Naidoo, Alison Coyle
Designer Claudia Balderrama
Photographers Tim Connolly, Mark Heriot
Stylists Jeanette Thompson, Peach Panfili

National Library of Australia Cataloguing-in-Publication data

Wonderful Appliqué Quilts

Includes index
ISBN 1 875625 31 3

1. Quilting

Printed by KHL Printing Co, Singapore

Australian distribution to supermarkets and newsagents by Network Distribution Company, 54 Park Street, Sydney NSW 2000. Phone (02) 9282 8777.
Australian book shop distribution by Gary Allen Book Distribution, 9 Cooper Street, Smithfield NSW 2164. Phone (02) 9725 2933.
Overseas distribution enquiries Godfrey Vella. Phone 61 (2) 9748 0599. Locked Bag 111, Silverwater NSW 1811 Australia.
email: gvella@expresspublications.com.au web site: www.expresspublications.com.au